THE ENGLISH SPRINGER SPANIEL

Tammy Gagne

Project Team
Editor: Craig Sernotti
Copy Editor: Joann Woy
Indexer: Joann Woy
Design: Patricia Escabi
Series Design: Stephanie Krautheim and Mada Design
Series Originator: Dominique De Vito

T.F.H. Publications
President/CEO: Glen S. Axelrod
Executive Vice President: Mark E. Johnson
Publisher: Christopher T. Reggio
Production Manager: Kathy Bontz

T.F.H. Publications, Inc.
One TFH Plaza
Third and Union Avenues
Neptune City, NJ 07753

Printed and bound in China
10 11 12 13 14   3 5 7 9 8 6 4 2

Library of Congress Cataloging-in-Publication Data
Gagne, Tammy.
  The English springer spaniel / Tammy Gagne.
     p. cm.
  Includes index.
  ISBN 978-0-7938-3686-4 (alk. paper)
  1. English springer spaniels. I. Title.
SF429.E7G27 2009
636.752'4--dc22
                         2008034322

The Leader In Responsible Animal Care For Over 50 Years!®
www.tfh.com

TABLE OF CONTENTS

HISTORY

of the English Springer Spaniel

The English Springer Spaniel has been winning the hearts and praise of dog lovers around the world for over a century. Originally bred for their remarkable talent for flushing wild game, Springers also are known for their elegant good looks. The breed is no stranger to the show ring. For these reasons, it may be easy to assume that the gun dog variety and the bench show type are two separate, albeit closely related breeds. After all, seldom does one see this kind of versatility in a single dog breed. However, the hunting type and the show dog variety are indeed two distinct members of this same multifaceted breed.

EARLY DEVELOPMENT OF THE BREED

Unlike many other dog breeds, there is little question as to the heritage of the English Springer Spaniel. The Springer's name alone denotes both countries of this breed's clear-cut origins. First, England lays claim to her beautiful Springer with the word "English." Second, the word "spaniel" is derived from the French phrase *Chiens de l'Espagnol*, which means "dog of Spain." Spaniels were most likely brought from Spain to England with the Romans. Since the Springer was introduced to England more than 2,000 years ago, though, it is safe to say the Springer is now a true Brit.

Known for flushing (or "springing") birds for hunters, Springers were labeled "land

English Springer Spaniels are active, loyal dogs.

A New Game Plan

Before the invention of firearms, spaniels worked in conjunction with birds of prey in hunting with their owners. The role of the bird, usually a hawk or a falcon, was to keep the game on the ground by flying threateningly overhead. The spaniel would then track and flush these smaller birds so that the hunter could capture them with a net. In the seventeenth century, shotguns rendered the hawks and falcons obsolete, but the spaniels could not be replaced. These prodigious gun dogs are still the sole companion of the modern-day game hunter.

Spaniels." Other descendants of these early Spaniels instead offered a talent for retrieving birds from water and were thus called "water Spaniels." These include breeds known today as the Irish Water Spaniel and the American Water Spaniel.

Whether an English Springer Spaniel resides on the east or west side of the Atlantic, he is known across the board as the English Springer Spaniel. This is in part due to the presence of another Springer: the Welsh Springer Spaniel. This close relation to the English Springer was developed, as its name states, in Wales. The two breeds share many qualities, including predispositions to certain health issues. They differ, however, in both color and temperament. The English Springer is said to have put the "spring" into the English Springer breed. Welsh Springers are known for being significantly calmer dogs.

BREED HISTORY IN ENGLAND

A Brave Companion

William Wallace, the Scottish hero portrayed by Mel Gibson in the movie *Braveheart*, was said to have owned a Springer Spaniel named Merlin MacDonald. According to legend, this dog served his country alongside Wallace in the defeat of the English army in the Battle of Stirling Bridge.

The Springer is the foundation for most of the spaniel breeds we know today. At one time, Springer Spaniels, Sussex Spaniels, and Cocker Spaniels were all born within the same litters. Size alone made the differentiations between these breeds. This system proved problematic, however, when bench shows (early versions of contemporary dog shows) began. A dog might have been entered into competition one year as a Cocker Spaniel, but due to continued growth, this same dog would then be classified as a Springer Spaniel the following year. Additionally, a so-called Springer could have either Cockers or Sussex Spaniels in his immediate pedigree, further complicating the breed boundaries.

At the beginning of the nineteenth century, Aqualane Kennels in Shropshire, England, began striving to standardize the

Springer Spaniel's characteristics. Owned by the Boughey family, Aqualane owned Springers dating back to 1812. Many modern-day English Springer Spaniels can be traced back to the Boughey's dogs: Mop I, Mop II, and Frisk. The Spaniel Club in England was formed in 1885. Its members created the first true breed standards for the various breeds of spaniels.

BREED HISTORY IN THE U.S.

In 1880 the American Spaniel Club was formed. This organization soon declared that any dog weighing more than 28 pounds (13 kg) would be considered a Springer, and fanciers stopped breeding the various sizes together. In 1902, England's Kennel Club (KC) also granted Springers and Cockers separate breed status. As one breeder told me, "It is fun to follow a champion Springer's pedigree back until you hit Cockers."

The American Kennel Club (AKC) officially recognized the English Springer Spaniel in 1910, when they registered a female dog named Denne Lucy. In 1922, a group of sportsmen in the United States formed the English Springer Spaniel Field Trial Association (ESSFTA). Although the focus of this organization is, as the name states, field dogs, the AKC has recognized the ESSFTA as the parent club and primary authority for the breed since 1927.

In the American Kennel Club (AKC), the English Springer Spaniel is part of the sporting group. In England's Kennel Club (KC), though, the Springer belongs to the gundog group, the KC's version of our sporting group.

The English Springer Spaniel (left) and Welsh Springer Spaniel (right) share many qualities, but the English Springer is a more lively breed than the Welsh Springer.

AKC—A Dog Registry and More

Far more than a registry for purebred dog breeds, the AKC organizes scores of events for purebred dog lovers. Look for English Springer Spaniels in the Westminster Kennel Club Dog Show, an annual event sponsored by the AKC in New York City, or attend a regional event closer to your home town. Not into conformation? Consider attending an AKC-sanctioned obedience trial or an agility competition. Your dog needn't even be a purebred Springer to participate in either of these pastimes. The AKC is also an active participant in tracking dog-related legislation across the country, lobbying against laws that its members feel would be detrimental to the canine species, and supporting legislation that can better life for all dogs.

At the turn of the century, well-bred Springers competed successfully in both field trials and conformation events. Shortly thereafter, however, the breed began to diverge in type. As showing became more popular both here and in the UK, the look of the English Springer Spaniel began to change. Show dogs were being bred to be heavier and stockier than their gundog cousins, and their coats were becoming more profuse—qualities that made it increasingly difficult for dogs to excel in the field. Other noticeable changes included

The English Springer Spaniel's popularity was never as high as other spaniels, but it is very popular among hunters as a gun dog.

longer ears and a slightly different shape to the dome of the show Springer's head.

Field dogs continued to be bred for their acute sense of smell, speed, and endurance. Bench-style Springers, on the other hand, were becoming a bit slower due to their heavier-boned construction. This also limited their stamina, although both types retained the breed's hunting instinct. Bench-style Springers can still be trained for hunting, although field dogs usually demonstrate greater overall ability.

In 1906, a liver and white Springer owned by F. Winton Smith became the first English Springer Spaniel champion ever. His name was Beechgrove Will. Other notable champions included Ch. Rivington Sam (whose mother was a registered Cocker Spaniel), and dual champions Flint of Avendale and Horsford Hetman. Most breeders believe the days of dual champions are now over, though. The last dual champion in the breed was Green Valley Punch, who achieved the distinction in 1938.

The English Springer Spaniel's popularity in the United States soared from the early to mid-1900s, as the country's pheasant population also grew in record numbers. The Springer was, and still is, considered the quintessential gun dog by many American bird hunters. Fortunately for the English Springer Spaniel, demand for the breed never matched that for the American Cocker—a frenzied fame that led to inbreeding, overbreeding, and a multitude of subsequent problems. The Springer's more conservative popularity helped keep the breed free of many of the tribulations faced by the Cocker.

First Dogs

In 1989, a litter of English Springer Spaniel puppies was born in the White House. The dam was Millie, the dog of then President George H. W. Bush. One of Millie's puppies, a dog named Spot, returned to her birthplace when her master, George W. Bush, took office in 2000.

Best in Show Favorite

Since 1993, the English Springer Spaniel has won the prestigious title of Best in Show at the Westminster Kennel Club Dog Show three separate years. A male Springer by the name of Ch. Salilyn's Condor took the title in 1993. This dog's daughter, Ch. Salilyn-N-Erin's Shameless, then earned the trophy in 2000. A third Springer, Ch. Felicity's Diamond Jim (known to many as James), added yet another Best in Show win for the breed in 2007.

C h a p t e r

2

CHARACTERISTICS
of the English Springer Spaniel

I f one were to describe the English Springer Spaniel in a single word, the word
would likely be "versatile." A Springer may be a skilled hunter or a
championship show dog. Although most Springers fall into one category or the
other—field or bench-style—each of these types is part of the same amazing
breed. In addition to these impressive roles, the Springer is also known for
being a faithful companion. Whether you prefer a hunting dog, a conformation
contender, or just a lovable pet, this breed is sure to please.

PHYSICAL DESCRIPTION

When many people think of the English Springer Spaniel, they picture a medium-
sized black and white dog. And while many Springers do indeed fit this description,
the breed also comes in liver (brown) and white, as well as in both color combinations
with additional tan markings, commonly called tan points. Ticking, or freckles, may or
may not be present in the white areas. Springers may also be blue roan or liver roan,
meaning that the dog has dark hairs growing in the white sections of his coat. A blue
roan has black hairs scattered among the white sections, whereas a liver roan has
brown hairs in these areas. Occasionally, a Springer may be lemon, red, or orange in
color, but none of these colors is allowed in the show ring.

Unless you plan to show your dog, the color and arrangements of his markings are
truly arbitrary. Even in the ring, markings are not supposed to be judged at all. A
Springer with loads of freckles or one with almost solid coloring is technically as
correct as one with a dark blanket and a white collar blaze—and one is just as likely as
any other to make a wonderful pet.

Field dogs are not held to the same aesthetic standards as show dogs. Springers
used for hunting tend to be more open-coated (meaning they have larger white areas)
than bench-style Springers. Show dogs tend to have solid blankets of color on their
backs, whereas a field dog's back is often spotted. Breeders of show-style Springers
strive for a more consistent look in their dogs than do breeders of field Springers.
Whereas a show dog's hair is left long and profuse, a field dog's coat is typically
clipped shorter and requires far less maintenance. Breeders of the latter type insist that

A Springer of a Different Color

When roan puppies are born, they look just like regular black and white or liver and white dogs. During the first few hours of their lives, though, the skin beneath a roan puppy's coat turns a grayish color. Due to their darker coloring, blue roans are usually easier to identify shortly after birth, but it can take a few weeks for a breeder to be certain whether any pup is indeed a roan. A roan's solid white hair will grow out gradually over the first year. This is replaced with new white hair that is heavily ticked with either black or liver.

So, how do you tell the difference between a roan Springer and a dog whose hair is merely ticked? Roan Springers carry a dominant gene for this coat pattern; a roan dog must have a roan parent. The roan coat is dominant over both regular ticked and nonticked coats.

while their dogs may not look as fancy as bench dogs, their talent more than makes up for their lack of fancy sparkle.

Ears and Eyes

The signature English Springer Spaniel ears are long and wide. A show dog's ear leather should be long enough to reach the tip of his nose. The Springer's oval eyes are set wide apart and should match the dog's coloring. Liver and white dogs typically have hazel eyes, whereas the eyes of black and white dogs are usually dark brown to black. The eyes set level with the ears on the dog's skull.

Profile

The Springer's neck is moderately long and slightly arched, leading to sloping shoulders. Legs are muscular with well-developed hips and thighs. The back is straight and strong. It is

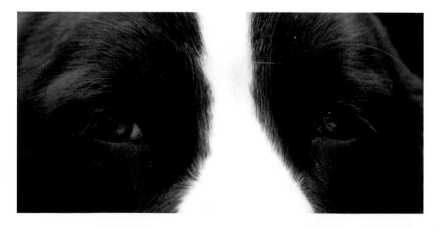

A Springer's eyes should always be alert, clear, and clean.

essentially level, but does slant slightly from the withers to the dog's tail. This affords the Springer with his instantly recognizable profile.

One thing most show and field Springers do have in common is a docked tail. The original purpose of docking was to make it easier for this breed to make its way through brush while hunting. If left long, the Springer's naturally long tail can be a detriment in the field if it gets caught on vegetation. Although docking a show dog's tail has no such purpose, the practice is still currently done by most English Springer Spaniel breeders in the United States. Considered both cruel and unnecessary by its opponents, however, tail docking has been made illegal in numerous other countries around the world—with exceptions granted to dogs used for hunting. The United States may likely adopt similar legislation at some point in the future, as many Americans also oppose this long-standing practice.

Size

The differences between a show dog's and a field dog's appearance reach far beyond their coats. Show-style Springers typically measure between 19 and 20 inches (48 to 51 cm) tall and weigh between 40 and 50 pounds (18 to 23 kg). They are slighter longer than they are tall. Field dogs fall into a much wider size range—from slightly smaller than show dogs to much larger. Field dogs also tend to be longer-bodied than bench Springers. Some breeders have noticed a growing trend to add bone structure to the bench-style dogs, and they fear it could make them clumsy and awkward. Lighter-boned field Springers have greater endurance.

A Wonderful Dog

Both field and show Springers are athletic dogs, filled with obvious enthusiasm. The American Kennel Club (AKC) breed standard describes the English Springer Spaniel as "a sporting dog of distinct spaniel character, combining beauty and utility." A Springer in motion is indeed a spectacular sight, made even more beautiful by the instinctual purpose behind his movements. Whether working in the field or strutting his stuff in the ring, an English Springer Spaniel exudes both power and agility.

What Is a Breed Standard?

For each breed eligible for AKC registration, an official breed standard exists. Created by the breed's parent club, this description of an ideal dog is used as a guideline for the judging of conformation events. It also serves as a model for breeders. Although the standard describes the perfect dog, very rarely does such a faultless dog exist.

Which Dog Makes the Better Pet—a Bench Springer or a Field Springer?

Before starting your search for an English Springer Spaniel, you must decide which type of Springer best suits your lifestyle. For many decades, Springer breeders have focused their energies on either conformation or field work. If you wish to utilize the breed's aptitude for hunting, your decision between the two will be an easy one. Likewise, a bench-type Springer is the clear choice if you wish to show your dog. But what if you want a Springer primarily as a companion animal? Which one is best then? The easiest way to find the right dog for you is to talk to breeders. These are the people who know English Springer Spaniels best, and they can help you decide which type matches your individual personality and daily routine.

TEMPERAMENT AND BEHAVIOR

The English Springer Spaniel is a very smart and dynamic breed. Consequently, Springers need constant activity to keep their sharp minds busy and to channel their fierce energy. If you don't train your Springer to behave properly, he will inevitably learn less desirable behaviors on his own. Field Springers usually have more energy than bench dogs. The latter type is said to be more laid back, but they too are more active than many other breeds. Breeders say sometimes this eagerness for activity can be mistaken for a hyperactive personality, but observing a Springer within the home reveals a well-balanced proportion of motion and stillness.

Springers can also be very sensitive. For this reason, while training must be consistent, it must never be harsh. A harsh admonishment can destroy a puppy's (or even an adult's) confidence. This can hamper future success with training and socialization.

Well-adjusted Springers possess a strong desire for achievement. Whether they are trotting around the show ring, hunting birds, or learning a new obedience command, Springers want to do whatever it takes to please their owners. This is an incredibly loyal breed. If you are looking for a guard dog, though, an English Springer Spaniel probably isn't the dog for you. As one breeder told me, "A Springer will alert you to a stranger but then show him to your silver—and of course, the dog treats."

PET SUITABILITY

Because the English Springer Spaniel is such a versatile breed, almost any type of Springer fancier can find a dog who matches his or her individual lifestyle. Perhaps you are an active city dweller who walks to work and enjoys hiking on the weekends. Or maybe you are a stay-at-home dad who lives in the suburbs and spends weekends at your kids' soccer games. Most Springers can easily adapt to either way of life.

City or Country?

If you live in the city, owning an English Springer Spaniel can be a much more complicated undertaking. The simple act of finding housing that allows dogs can be a challenge for many urban owners. Although some apartments and condominiums allow pets, many only allow cats or smaller dog breeds. If you live in a high-rise building, the logistics of taking a Springer inside and outside several times each day can be both time-consuming and tiring, even if you use an elevator.

Owners living in rural areas or the suburbs may find it much easier to own this active breed. Most suburban neighborhoods are a virtual roadmap for daily dog walks. If you live even further outside the city, you may have quick access to great

Home Is Where Your Springer Is

Whether you live in the city or the suburbs, finding a place to live can be a challenge if you own a dog. An overwhelming number of apartment buildings have strict no-pet policies. It's not just pet-owning renters who are affected. Many condominiums and neighborhood associations also impose rules restricting dog ownership. If you are searching for a new home for you and your English Springer Spaniel, several websites can help you find pet-friendly housing. Some even offer listings for hotels and vacation homes that accept canine guests.

www.fidofriendly.com

www.peoplewithpets.com

www.petsok.com

www.petrent.net

www.petvacationhomes.com

If you have an active outdoor lifestyle, an English Springer Spaniel may be the right dog for you.

You Can Take the Springer Out of the City—but Not the Country!

If you choose to move out of the city, your Springer will easily adapt to suburban or rural life. A dog raised in the country, however, may have a hard time adjusting to city life.

hiking trails, state parks, and other recreational areas. Just be sure that dogs are allowed before heading out the door.

Children

With the English Springer Spaniel's perpetual energy, Springers and kids can be an ideal combination. Even a young parent may be hard-pressed to keep up with a lively eight-year-old the way this breed can. What's more, most Springers love children. Perhaps they have noticed that children approach life with much the same enthusiasm and curiosity as they do. Kids find even the more mundane aspects of dog ownership, like brushing and bathing, a whole lot of fun—and they can make them more fun for your dog, as well. Who better to praise your Springer puppy for going potty outside, after all, than a preschooler who just recently mastered potty training herself?

It is imperative that both Springers and children are taught how to properly respect each other. For your Springer, this means no jumping up or nipping, even if it is done in play. For your child, showing respect means always being gentle with your Springer, never trying to sneak up on him or startle him, and using positive reinforcement only. Adult supervision should always be part of the Springer–child equation, but

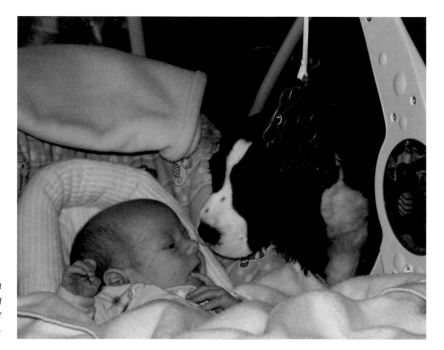

Any interactions between your dog and young children should always be closely monitored by you.

Kidding Around

When exposed to each other early on, Springers and children usually become fast friends. Whether you have kids of your own or not, introduce your dog to children by making them part of his earliest socialization. Encourage young people to gently pat your Springer or offer him healthy treats while out walking or playing at the park, and he will soon associate these smaller humans with rewards. If you have kids of your own, include them in training and caring for your new pet. Even toddlers can help with small tasks, such as praising the dog when he follows a command or carrying a can of food to the counter at meal time. As your son or daughter gets older and more responsible, you can expand the number and types of tasks you delegate. Even older children and dogs with the sweetest temperaments, however, should always be supervised when together.

when raised together, most Springers get along remarkably well with kids.

It is important to point out, though, that every dog has his own temperament and personality. If your Springer reacts poorly to sudden movements or loud noises, being around children can be problematic. Small children are frequently loud and animated. Likewise, if your dog acts aggressively around people, interactions with children cannot be allowed. If you are dealing with aggression, talk to your Springer's veterinarian for advice.

Other Household Pets

Most English Springer Spaniels get along well with fellow Springers and other dogs. While Springers aren't pack hunters, they possess a loving and accepting nature that helps them fit into most multi-dog families, which mimic pack dynamics. Cats, too, are usually fine choices for household companions for Springers. Birds and rodents, though, will not be safe sharing a house with this breed. A Springer's hunting instincts are simply too strong. Even a birdfeeder can be a bad idea if you own a Springer. "I think the fun lies in the chase, though, and not in actual demise of any such animals," explained one breeder.

Dominant Males

Male Springers sometimes compete for dominance over each other. While many owners try to treat each dog the same, canine pack structure simply doesn't work this way. In virtually any

Springers are natural hunters. Keeping one in the same house with birds or small rodents is therefore probably not a good idea.

household, whether there are two dogs or more, one dog is indeed the dominant animal. Unless your Springers are acting too aggressively with each other, this is a situation in which it is best to let the dogs settle the issue themselves. If it is clear that a particular dog is the dominant one, you can make things easier by treating him just a little differently from the rest. Feed him first, for instance, or take him for his morning walk before the others. This can help to maintain harmony in your household pack.

Dominant Females

A female Springer may also hold a dominant spot in your canine family, especially if she arrived before any other dogs in the home. To avoid problems with pack order, look for submissive puppies when adding a canine family member to your household. It truly can make all the difference in the how easily the new addition settles into your family.

Exercise Needs

Springers require lots of exercise, but this does not mean that owners must have large backyards equipped with expensive fences or other containment systems. All owners must make the effort, however, to get their Springers outside for regular and adequate playtime. For urban owners, this often means trekking across town to a dog park or other canine-friendly area daily. The willingness to provide your Springer with a routine filled with fresh air and exercise is much more important than whether you live in the suburbs or on the twenty-seventh floor of a high-rise building.

When many dog owners think of exercising their pets, they think of daily walks. This is a great start, but unfortunately, it is not enough for most English Springer Spaniels. Field dogs in particular have seemingly boundless energy, but even a bench-style Springer needs regular time and space to run. Given the opportunity, many Springers can remain active all day long.

Regular off-leash time (in a safe environment) is a great way for many dogs to release pent-up energy. Springers love chasing and retrieving balls. Many also enjoy swimming or jogging. Field dogs can get additional exercise through hunting. Other Springers enjoy participating in organized events, such as agility or flyball.

If left indoors with nothing to do all day, Springers are more likely to develop problem behaviors, like chewing or howling. A well-exercised Springer, on the other hand, will spend his indoor time resting. As one breeder told me, "Be prepared to run for the gold during the day with this breed, but at night fluff up your couch."

The Omega Dog

When my husband and I chose our male Spaniel, Damon, it was clear from the beginning that he would fill the role of the omega dog. When he played with his littermates at the breeder's home, his was always the first puppy belly turned upward, the canine gesture for surrender. Power and control mean nothing to Damon. He is more than happy to sit and wait for either attention or treats. He delights in both, but we have shown him that waiting his turn never means going without. This has made him completely secure with his position in the family, even if it is the lowest spot in the hierarchy.

3

PREPARING
for Your English Springer Spaniel

O nce you decide that an English Springer Spaniel is in your future, the next step is finding the dog for you. Perhaps you want to raise your Springer from a puppy, or maybe you want to rescue an adult Springer in need of a new home. Whichever choice you make, some preparations for your new family member are in order. So, which supplies should make up that all-important first shopping list? What other items should you consider? In the beginning, all the choices and questions can seem overwhelming, but by taking your time and planning ahead, you can help ensure that your Springer will make the transition into his new home as smoothly as possible.

THE AGE-OLD QUESTION

It's easy to understand why so many people choose to buy English Springer Spaniel puppies. In addition to being adorable, each of these energetic little bundles of joy is poised at the starting line of a long and happy lifetime. Puppies also come with a clean slate. They have no deeply ingrained behavior problems, they haven't been mistreated by previous owners, and all you have to do to learn more about your pup's ancestry is reach for his pedigree. Still, adopting an adult Springer has clear advantages. Most adult dogs are already housetrained and well past the teething phase. Older dogs also have established temperaments. For many people, older dogs make even better pets than young puppies. Whichever you choose, welcoming an English Springer Spaniel into your home is sure to be a rewarding experience.

Although puppyhood doesn't last long, it can be a mighty demanding time in a dog's life. Much like young children, puppies are incredibly impressionable beings. Their most formative time periods all lie within the first two years of their lives. This means that making time for their training and socialization is of utmost importance. If realistically you don't have that time or the patience these tasks require, an older dog may be a better fit for you. Adult Springers often are also better choices for families with younger children, providing the dog has had positive experiences with kids in his past.

Training your dog while he is still a puppy will help him become a well-behaved adult.

If, on the other hand, you anxiously await taking your Springer to puppy kindergarten and being an integral part of his early training, a puppy may be ideal for you. Perhaps you have just lost a beloved, older companion to illness and simply want to put as many years as possible between now and when you have to say goodbye to another pet. This is also a perfectly understandable reason for preferring a younger Springer. The good news is that there are no hard and fast rules regarding age. The key to choosing the right dog is choosing the right one *for you.*

SHOW DOG OR FIELD DOG?

Another important consideration in selecting an English Springer Spaniel is deciding between a bench-style Springer or a field dog. Neither is necessarily better than the other, but the two types can be drastically different. Although a small number of Springers have both field dogs and bench dogs in their pedigrees, most breeders prefer to preserve the traits of each type rather than trying to combine the two. If you are an avid hunter and want a passionate helper, a field Springer is likely your better option. If you love the look of the English Springer Spaniels you've seen on television competing in conformation, though, a show-style dog sounds more like your cup of tea. Just because you prefer the feathered coat and long ears does not mean you have to show your pet, though. Many show-quality dogs make wonderful companions for those who care little about blue ribbons and championship titles.

WHERE TO FIND THE DOG OF YOUR DREAMS

Once you decide that an English Springer Spaniel is in your future, the next step is finding the dog of your dreams. What's the best way to find a reputable breeder? What types of guarantees should you expect? If adopting, will you have to jump through all sorts of hoops before you can take your Springer home? Do rescues offer any follow-up resources for new owners?

Breeders

Reputable breeders stand head and shoulders above the rest—once you meet them, that is. Unfortunately, they can be a bit harder to find, since few truly regard breeding as a business. The best breeders are often called "hobby breeders," because they raise dogs first and foremost for the betterment of the breed. Their commitment to striving for the very best health and temperament is evident in their limited number of litters each year, as well as in their tendency to raise only one or two breeds. (A huge red flag when searching for a breeder is an advertisement for several different breeds with just one phone number!) Even after you find a good Springer breeder, you may still need to wait several months for a puppy. A handful of breeders offer both show-style Springers and dogs bred for working in the field. Most, however, prefer to specialize in one type of dog or the other.

A reputable breeder will answer all of your questions and will not make you feel foolish for asking them.

The Power of Three

Many English Springer Spaniel breeders insist that three is the magic number when it comes to their dogs. Most breeders will wait until a female is three years old before breeding her for the first time. By this age, a Springer is physically ready for pregnancy and delivery, frequently referred to as whelping. Additionally, a dog this age will have an established temperament and health history. Most genetic health problems that will ultimately occur in a Springer will have presented themselves by the age of three.

Also, female Springers should be bred no more frequently than once every three heat cycles. This usually leaves about 18 months minimum between litters. Just like a human's, the canine body must fully recuperate after a birth. Back-to-back litters are simply too much for any breed.

Finally, most reputable breeders will breed a female Springer no more than three times during her lifetime. Having too many litters can be stressful for a dog. After whelping three litters, most Springers are ready to be spayed and settle into a home as a beloved pet. If a female has an especially difficult time delivering pups, though, a good breeder will allow her to retire after just a single litter.

Price

Although a quality English Springer Spaniel can be pricey, I guarantee you a good breeder isn't making a killing on her dogs. Most are lucky to just break even by the time the last puppy from a litter finds a home. If the Springer puppy you have your eye on is the product of champions, a great investment of both time and money has been made to ensure that your puppy's parents possess all the traits an English Springer Spaniel should. The looks and temperaments of a puppy's parents are an extremely accurate indicator of how he will look and act once he is all grown up.

Attend Shows to Research Breeders

The show ring can in fact be an excellent starting point for finding your Springer puppy. Attending conformation shows and field trials are also excellent means of learning more about the English Springer Spaniel breed. If a particular dog grabs your attention, introduce yourself to the owner or handler once her turn is over. Most Springer owners love talking about their favorite subject: Springers. Ask any questions you may have, including the name of the breeder, and be sure to listen carefully to everything the person tells you. Many people who participate in these organized activities also breed dogs, so you may have just met the breeder of your future Springer puppy.

Visit the Breeder

A good breeder will welcome your visit, but you must understand that timing can be a crucial concern. If the breeder has a pregnant female or pups in the house, she may not allow any visitors until the puppies reach a certain age—usually around four weeks. This is not a sign of an unsavory breeder; on the contrary, it is a sign that you are dealing with someone who puts the welfare of her dogs first. Strangers can bring any number of diseases into the breeder's household. If you have been to a dog park recently, for example, you could have encountered the parvovirus, a highly contagious and dangerous canine disease that is spread through contact with infected feces. For this reason, the breeder may even ask you to remove your shoes before entering, since parvo can sometimes live in the ground for several months. Eventually, the breeder will immunize the pups against this deadly disease, but as long as they are too young for this inoculation, they are extremely vulnerable.

When you meet the breeder, listen to your gut. You certainly don't have to like her, but a good rapport is a definite plus. Don't let a strong personality scare you off. Some of the best breeders, even those who are naturally shy in most other areas of their lives, have become amazingly adept at protecting their dogs from undesirable owners. This too is a good thing. If you get a bad feeling, however, heed it. Often our initial instincts about a person or situation are the most reliable.

Inspect the Surroundings

Look around for signs that the dogs are in good hands. Are both the dogs and their space clean? Don't fault a breeder for a little dust on the furniture or a cobweb in the corner. Remember, she has been busy caring for those pups! The dogs' accommodations also need not be fancy, but the mother and puppies should have at least a small area that is separate from the other dogs in the house. Do the adult dogs seem happy and healthy? Are they treated like part of the family?

Additional Breeder Resources

Other resources for finding good hobby breeders include your local veterinarian, humane society, and the American Kennel Club (AKC). The AKC's website, www.akc.org, includes a breeder referral link alongside the English Springer Spaniel's breed standard. The English Springer Spaniel Field Trial Association (ESSFTA) also offers a breeder referral page for both show and field dogs. Neither the AKC or the ESSFTA, though, can guarantee that a breeder is a good one. The best way to evaluate a Springer breeder is to request a personal visit.

A breeder's dogs should be clean and healthy, as should their surroundings.

Sires, Dams, and Pups

You may or may not be able to meet the puppies' sire, since many breeders use stud dogs belonging to other breeders. Once the breeding period is finished, the stud dog's job is done. Many Springer pups never meet their sires. Also, if no stud fee was paid, the owner of the stud usually gets the pick of the litter. This means she gets to take one puppy of her choice. If you decide you want a particular pup, this also means that you may need to wait a while to find out if he is in fact available.

Breeders keep certain pups for future breeding. When looking for a potential dam or sire, the breeder wants a dog who most closely matches the breed standard or one who shows potential as a field dog. Most often these qualities reveal themselves over time. A breeder may not decide which, if any, of the pups she is keeping until the dogs are several weeks old for this reason. A breeder may even keep a puppy and ultimately elect not to breed him at all.

The dam should be friendly and well socialized. The breeder should have paperwork stating that both of the parents' hips, elbows, and eyes have been checked and cleared by the appropriate agencies. The Orthopedic Foundation of America (OFA), which certifies hips and elbows, uses several different ratings. These include excellent, good, and fair. A dog without one of these ratings should not be bred. The eyes of both the parents and the pups should be checked by a veterinarian who is a member of the American College of Veterinary Ophthalmologists (ACVO). A puppy must be at least seven weeks old at the time of his eye exam for the results to be reliable. If the puppy you choose is still younger than this, be sure to follow-up on this information later.

Testing for PRA

A revolutionary test for the mutated gene that causes progressive retinal atrophy (PRA) in Springers is now available. Since this eye disease causes irreversible blindness, being able to test dogs for this gene before breeding them is an invaluable preventive measure. Ideally, both parents should test "normal," meaning they do not possess the PRA gene. Unfortunately, a great number of Springers do possess at least one copy of the gene, so many breeders do elect to breed dogs dubbed "carriers." By breeding them to dogs testing normal, however, the breeders can reduce the likelihood of the puppies developing the problem. Out of the three possible results, testing "affected" is by far the worst scenario. This means a dog possesses two copies of the gene. Dogs who test affected have

New puppies must stay with their mothers and nurse for several weeks before they are ready to go home with their new owner.

The Perfect Spinger Puppy

When selecting a Springer puppy, look for one who comes to you right away when you sit on the floor. If he crawls all over you and showers you with kisses, all the better! After a few minutes, set him down to play with his littermates and watch his interactions with them. If you pick the shyest or the boldest puppy in the group, you should be prepared for a little extra work in the socialization or training department.

the greatest chance of developing the disease; an affected English Springer Spaniel may be as much as 20 times more likely to suffer from PRA than other Springers.

Put It in Writing

Most breeders offer a written warranty for each puppy they sell. They also typically require each buyer to sign an agreement, as well. The details of both forms can vary, but most promise a refund or replacement animal if the puppy you purchase develops problems with his hips or eyes within the first two years of ownership. A buyer agreement may require you to notify the breeder if at any point you cannot keep the dog. Breeders don't want their puppies ending up in shelters or rescue organizations. If you need to find your dog a new home, most breeders will take an active role in this process to ensure the best possible outcome.

It is important to remember, however, that a warranty is not a guarantee. Two dogs with excellent hip ratings can, in rare cases, produce a puppy who develops hip dysplasia. Any dog can in fact develop any kind of health problem at any time.

Adoption

When it comes to finding an English Springer Spaniel, adoption is without a doubt the most overlooked option. Many people simply don't realize that many purebred dogs are available through breed rescue groups—and even at their local animal shelters. Also, don't assume that all dogs in need of new homes are part of the senior set. You can find young adult dogs and sometimes even puppies in need of adoption.

You may also call your local humane society to let them know you are actively searching for an English Springer Spaniel. If no Springers are available for adoption at this time, leave your name and number and ask someone to let you know if one comes into the shelter.

Price

Going the route of adoption doesn't mean you will pay nothing for your Springer. Most shelters and rescue groups charge a small fee to help with the cost of running their organizations. Also, nearly all dogs placed in this way are required to be spayed or neutered prior to going home with their new owners. Often local veterinarians volunteer to perform these sterilizations at a discounted rate, resulting in a nominal charge passed on to the new owner.

The Adoption Process

Dealing with a breed rescue group can feel a little intimidating at first. It may even seem a bit like the process for adopting a child instead of a pet. People involved in rescue can be quite passionate about their work. They want the very best for the dogs they place. Most importantly, they want each dog's next home to be his last. This makes the approval process paramount.

After filling out an adoption application, you will then schedule a home visit. Someone from the breed rescue will arrive at your home at a mutually convenient time. All household members should attend this meeting, including kids and any other pets you may own. The actual visit is almost always less stressful than the adoptive family anticipates. All the rescue worker wants to do is meet you in person and make sure the setting is right for the Springer you will be adopting. Matching the right dog with the right people is perhaps the most important step in the adoption process.

You may also need to provide references before being approved. Veterinarians and other people involved in the animal community top the list of desirable choices, but friends and co-workers can also serve this purpose. Depending on the temperament, energy level, and history of the Springer you choose, the rescue may also require that you have a certain amount of experience with dogs, or even with Springers in particular. This, too, is in everyone's

Adopt From a Breeder

If you are looking for an adult Springer, a breeder is still one of your best resources. Many breeders are involved with rescue and can point you in an excellent direction. The breeder may even be looking to retire one of her former dams or sires, placing the dog with a new family. Your perfect Springer may be a dog the breeder had originally planned to use in her program. If an adult Springer doesn't match the breed standard as closely as the breeder predicted, the breeder may try to place him as a pet instead of breeding him.

best interest. Both you and the rescue worker must be confident that you can meet all your dog's needs.

Ownership Agreement

Like breeders, rescue groups require each new owner to sign an ownership agreement. Most agreements state that if you ever decide to give up the dog, the rescue organization will take it back. Even if you find what you think is a suitable home for the dog, you must surrender the dog back to the rescue. You may, of course, refer anyone interested in the dog to the rescue, but it is the rescue's job to evaluate new potential owners. By signing the agreement, you may also promise to always keep your dog on a leash in public and to clean up after him properly. Rescues want their adoptive families to be responsible dog owners, and they can get quite detailed about what defines that responsibility.

Support

Many dogs are available for adoption, including English Springer Spaniels.

If you adopt a Springer through rescue, the volunteers will continue to support you even after you bring your new pet home. Follow-up programs, like advice on transitioning and training, are regular parts of the rescue process. The volunteers want to make the adoption process go as smoothly as possible for both you and your new dog. Don't be afraid to turn to them if you need a little help.

Pet Stores

Pet stores sell a variety of purebred puppies. For this reason, they can be a convenient option for someone anxious to find an English Springer Spaniel. Potential owners must be extremely careful when dealing with these

Puppy Mills and Backyard Breeders

Investigative news stories about puppy mills regularly make national headlines. These large-scale commercial dog breeders produce animals purely for profit. Females are bred as soon as they are old enough to bear puppies, and they are repeatedly used to churn out litter after litter, with little regard to the animals' health or well-being. Most of the dogs are kept in dirty, too-small cages piled several high. They are not exercised or socialized adequately or fed properly.

A puppy coming from a puppy mill may look remarkably normal, but the problems an owner may encounter with such an animal are numerous. Because they are confined to such tiny spaces for the first weeks of their lives, dogs coming from puppy mills can become downright claustrophobic. Many, understandably, have an irreversible fear of being crated. Some are extremely difficult to housetrain. Even if a puppy mill Springer accepts a crate, the housetraining advantages it offers may still be lost. If he has been forced to eat and sleep amid his own excrement while at the puppy mill, he won't be fazed by soiling this new environment.

A backyard breeder may have slightly better intentions than a puppy mill owner, but sadly, the results are often the same. Some backyard breeders start breeding dogs because they love a certain breed and think their dogs would make good parents. Unfortunately, most people lack the knowledge and experience necessary for selecting dogs who should indeed be bred. The results are puppies that do not match their breed standard at all—or worse, animals with poor temperaments. Any reputable breeder will tell you that a friendly, reliable temperament is the most important quality for which any breeder strives.

Some backyard breeders get into breeding thinking they will make a fast buck, but a rude awakening soon follows. Raising dogs is an extremely expensive endeavor. The cost of healthy food, regular veterinary care, and health clearances add up quickly. Many backyard breeders skip important steps in order to make ends meet. Before they know it, they often have more dogs than they can realistically handle. This can lead to unsavory living conditions for the animals, neglect, or even outright abuse.

The best way to shut down puppy mills and backyard breeders is by not buying puppies from them. The only way to be certain you are not buying a dog from one of these insidious sellers is to buy directly from a breeder and visit her kennel personally. If you suspect you are dealing with a puppy mill or backyard breeder, report your concerns to your local humane society or police department. Many deplorable breeding operations have been shut down in this way.

businesses, though. Puppies in pet stores are usually extremely well cared for, but since each store sells such a wide variety of breeds, the staff simply cannot be as knowledgeable as breeders about each particular dog breed. Often, the employees also know little or nothing about a specific dog's history. Even a full pedigree is usually only available to the owner once a dog is purchased.

If you consider buying your Springer from a pet store, ask as many questions as possible. How old is the puppy? Where was he bred? What is the name of the kennel? Although nearly all pet stores insist that they don't get their dogs from puppy mills or backyard breeders, many do—sometimes without even realizing it.

Make sure the Springer you are looking at is healthy. Healthy Springer puppies have bright, clear eyes and thick coats. They don't sneeze or have runny noses. If the puppy appears unhealthy in any way, keep looking. Unfortunately, not all signs of illness are obvious. Ask to see the puppy's vaccination record and certificates stating that his hips and eyes have been certified by the OFA and AVCO.

Most pet stores offer health warranties, but these are usually contingent upon a veterinary exam within the first 48 hours of ownership. If you plan to purchase a puppy, have this important appointment scheduled before you complete the sale. Also, be sure you understand exactly what the warranty promises. Many warranties only offer to replace a sick animal with a healthy one, not refund your money. Since pet store dogs are usually considerably more expensive than dogs sold by breeders, you could be out a substantial amount of money.

GENERAL HOME PREPARATION

Preparing your home for a new English Springer Spaniel involves many tasks. It may at first even seem a bit like preparing for a human infant's arrival. First, there is the matter of puppy-proofing your home. Second, there is the list of things you must buy. As long as you don't put off either of these jobs until the last minute, neither one should be as stressful or expensive as it may sound.

You must puppy-proof your home before bringing home your new dog.

Registering Your English Springer Spaniel

American Kennel Club (AKC): Registering your new English Springer Spaniel puppy with the AKC is an easy and fun task. Your breeder should provide you with the necessary form, which will include both the dam and sire's registration numbers, as well as with your puppy's number. You just need to fill in your name and address, along with the name you have chosen for your dog.

Most breeders require that their kennel name precede the puppy's name. For example, if the kennel's name is Son of a Gun, and you want to name your dog Billy, the full registered name would be written Son of a Gun's Billy. The full name cannot exceed 30 letters. Spaces between words, apostrophes, and hyphens are counted in this total. You may choose a longer name for your dog's AKC paperwork, such as Billy the Kid, but use just Billy for his nickname.

There is a $15 nonrefundable application fee for registration. You can mail this payment along with your completed paperwork to the AKC or register online at www.akc.org. There you will find detailed instructions, including a first-time user's guide and checklist for the organization's online registration service.

Kennel Club (KC): In England, the complete registration of a litter with the KC is the responsibility of the breeder. During this process, the breeder will also officially name all the puppies. Each buyer is provided with a registration certificate for the puppy, complete with a section for the transfer of ownership that should be returned to the KC after the sale. A buyer should make sure that the breeder has signed this section of the document before forwarding it to the KC.

Puppy-Proofing Your Home

Begin the puppy-proofing process by getting down to your Springer's level—literally. Looking at your home from your dog's perspective can help you quickly identify the dangers that may be lurking in unexpected places. The exposed nail under your favorite chair, the cord to your mini-blinds, the rip at the bottom of the screen door all become more obvious when inspected at eye level.

While your Springer is still a puppy, consider using safety gates to block off staircases or rooms you do not want your dog to enter. A crate will help contain your pet when you can't watch him, but he must have a certain amount of space in his new home that he can explore safely and freely. At the very least, you should puppy-proof one room in your home for your new family member.

Nothing teaches us to pick up our belongings and put them away better than having a puppy in the house. Shoes, purses, children's playthings, and a host of other personal items make wonderful chew toys for your dogs—or at least your Springer will think so if they are left out for him to claim. Not only will you be upset when your favorite things are destroyed, but many common household items can also pose dangers to your puppy. I once knew of a dog who ate an entire box of facial tissues. He had to have emergency surgery to have the contents removed from his digestive system. Don't let this happen to your Springer.

Preparing your home for your new Springer also means preparing your fellow household members. In some cases, new routines must be established. If the kids help Mom carry the groceries in every Friday afternoon, someone must now first place your Springer in his crate (or gate him in another room) if you typically leave the door open during this process. Food is often of special concern. Especially if there are young children in the house, make sure everyone understands that plates cannot be placed in areas where your dog can sample the cuisine. Eating cookies and potato chips will make your Springer fat, but eating chocolate or onions will make him sick.

SUPPLIES

When I was pregnant with my son, I bought nearly every new baby item going. His room was filled with clothes, toys, and countless items that promised to make parenthood easier. Sadly, he grew out of several outfits before ever having a chance to wear them, many of the toys bored him, and the majority of those things I thought I just couldn't live without proved to do little more than take up space.

Many dog owners make this same mistake. They enter the pet supply store and think being a good dog owner means giving their dog a bunch of trendy trifles. When considering a new item for your English Springer Spaniel, ask yourself one important question: Will I really use this? You must be brutally honest with yourself. Deep down, you will know if a purchase is more fun than functional. If you are on the fence, leave it behind. You can always go back and get it if you change your mind later, but you cannot return an oversized stuffed monkey that plays sounds from the rain forest when you squeeze his 'ail after your dog has slobbered over it for two minutes and then moved on to more appealing toys.

The things your Springer truly needs aren't numerous, but they are important. Begin with the items below and place any items that may catch your eye at the pet supply store on a later list. I like to think over new purchases for several days. In many cases, I totally forget about the item before it's time to go back to the store.

Stainless steel water and food bowls are the best option for your Springer.

Food and Water Dishes

One of the first things your English Springer Spaniel needs is a set of dishes. Buying dog dishes may sound like an easy task, but most owners are amazed by the vast selection that awaits them at most pet supply stores. Is one material any better than another? Are there any health concerns involved? The answer to both questions is yes.

While ceramic bowls can be extremely attractive, they are also highly breakable. Even more importantly, they also pose the risk of lead poisoning to your pet. If you decide to use ceramic dishes, be sure to buy high-fire or table-quality items made for human use, since these are guaranteed to be safe. Currently, no such standards exist for items made for pets.

Does My Springer Need Outerwear?

If you live in a colder climate, you may wonder if you should buy coats and boots for your English Springer Spaniel. We've all seen these items in pet supply stores, but do they really keep a dog warm?

Especially if you keep your Springer in a shorter pet clip, wearing a coat or sweater really can make a big difference in how his body responds to the cold. If you keep your dog in full coat, his fur alone may be enough to keep him warm, but he still may appreciate a coat when the temperature dips below freezing. If your dogs are anything like mine, they will want to spend as much time as they can outdoors — even when the air turns frigid. A warm coat can make their outside time both more enjoyable and more plentiful.

Some dogs tolerate wearing boots very well. Mine do not. If your Springer is part of the former group, investing in a set of boots for rain or snow may be a smart idea. In addition to keeping his feet warm, boots can also provide your dog with added traction on ice. A second option for Springers wary of galoshes is paw wax. This inventive product can be applied directly to your dog's paw pads and serves a dual purpose. Not only does it help prevent slipping, but it also provides a barrier between feet and toxic elements like salt and other de-icers. What's more, paw wax can protect your dog's feet throughout the year, so don't forget to apply some before walking your Springer on that hot summer pavement, too.

Plastic bowls are a popular choice among pet owners, since they are lightweight and inexpensive. Unfortunately, these too can pose a health risk to your Springer. Dogs who eat and drink from plastic dishes may suffer from a condition called plastic dish nasal dermatitis. Dogs who experience this sensitivity to plastic can actually lose the pigment in their noses and lips, sometimes permanently, as a result of coming into repeated contact with this material. The condition can also cause pain and swelling. Unfortunately, I have some experience with this problem, as my first Spaniel suffered from it. I ended up swapping to stainless steel, but the color in Jonathan's nose never returned.

Stainless steel dishes are by far the safest and most versatile choice. Unlike ceramic dishes, stainless steel bowls won't break if you accidentally drop them on your tile floor—or if your Springer decides to hurl one across the floor himself. While plastic is extremely vulnerable to chewing, even the strongest chewer will be hard pressed to ruin stainless steel. This rugged material is also extremely easy to clean.

I recommend investing in two sets of dishes for your Springer. This makes feeding time remarkably easier. Simply replace the dirty dishes with the clean ones after you fill them with fresh food and water. Stainless steel is also dishwasher safe—a must-have quality for any dish in my home.

Crate, Dog Bed, or Both?

Every English Springer Spaniel needs a place to sleep. Perhaps you plan to crate train your new dog. If so, the next step is selecting the right kennel. If, on the other hand, you prefer a dog bed to crate, you need to find a canine cot that your Springer will find more comfy than your own bed covers. Either way, it is extremely important that you select and purchase this item as early as possible. Allow your dog to spend just one night atop your own bed's cozy covers, and I assure you, you will be sleeping with insufficient leg room for many years to come.

Crates

At one time, buying a crate was a pretty simple endeavor. An owner merely had to select the right size, and that was it. Now, however, the options and amenities are numerous. You may choose from wire crates, plastic crates, soft-sided crates—even crates with heating and cooling features. Like the crates themselves, liners are also available in a variety of styles and fabrics. Which one is best for you? The answer depends both on your lifestyle and your individual dog.

Establish boundaries and rules for your Springer Spaniel. If you don't want him on your furniture, do not allow him to jump up onto it when he is a puppy. If you are fine with your dog on the couch, though, covering it with a blanket will make cleaning much easier.

Is your dog a social butterfly? If so, he may prefer a wire crate, since it offers him a 360-degree view of his surroundings. Placing the crate in a high-traffic spot in your home, like the kitchen, can also help your social Springer feel more a part of the family action, even when he must be crated. If, on the other hand, your dog prefers a quieter retreat, consider a plastic kennel. Plastic is also a better choice for owners who plan to travel with their pets. Most airlines require these rigid-style kennels for canine travelers.

Soft-sided crates are usually made of nylon and collapse easily for quick storage. A crate like this may provide your Springer with a private refuge, but its flimsy design makes it a poor choice for dogs who chew or owners who wish to close the door. It simply isn't strong enough to contain a dog of his size.

Speaking of size, an intermediate crate (approximately 36 inches [90 cm] long) is best for this breed. If you go too small, your dog will feel cramped. If you go too big, he may use one end of the kennel as an impromptu bathroom. While your Springer is still a puppy, you may have to block off one end of the crate for this reason. Ideally, a dog should be able to stand, turn around, and lie down comfortably in his crate.

Crate Liner

When selecting a crate liner, look for something at least 2 inches (5 cm) thick. Fleece is a common choice for its softness and durability. Most importantly, select a liner that is machine washable. Buying two can also make laundry day a little less stressful. Simply toss the dirty liner in the hamper and replace it with the clean one.

Bed

If you want to provide your Springer with a bed of his own, you have many choices. Shape and fabric are largely matters of personal preference, but do look for a bed that is large enough for your dog to stretch out on comfortably. If it isn't big enough, he won't use it.

Like a crate liner, a dog bed should be easy to clean. Look for a cover that can zip off and be tossed into the washing machine for easy laundering. (Some manufacturers even hide the zipper when closed to deter chewers.) Also, make sure you know what

Blankets as a Bed or Crate Liner

If your Springer is still a puppy, you may want to postpone investing in a bed until your dog can be trusted not to chew or soil it. An old blanket or comforter can work well in the meantime. Just fold it a few times and place it where your dog's bed will go. A blanket can also serve as a temporary crate liner.

is inside the bed. Beds filled with cedar shavings may be comfortable, but they can be rough on a sensitive nose—either your Springer's or your own. Better choices include memory foam, shredded foam, and hypoallergenic fiberfill.

Leash and Collar

Your English Springer Spaniel's leash should be strong but not heavy. Nylon and cotton are good fabric choices. Both are available in a wide variety of colors and designs, but nylon tends to wear slightly better. Leather leads wear even better than nylon ones, but they are also more expensive.

The leash you select should be long enough to allow your Springer to walk comfortably alongside you. If you plan to walk your Springer primarily in busy areas like crowded streets and city sidewalks, a 4-foot (1.2-m) length is best. A shorter lead like this is also preferable for teaching a puppy how to walk on a leash. Longer leashes offer too much freedom during this behavior-shaping period. When taking your adult Springer for his everyday walks, a 6-foot (1.8-m) leash is usually more comfortable. Additional length will come in quite handy, however, for training a dog or teaching him to come when called. At your local pet supply store, you will find a variety of leashes from 4 to 24 feet (1.2 to 7.3 m) or longer.

I recommend investing in a retractable lead. This versatile item is literally several leashes in one. An owner may use it at its shortest length (usually about 4 feet [1.2 m]), its longest (typically about 16 feet [4.9 m]), or anywhere in between. Retractable leashes can be extremely handy when walking a dog

Teach your dog how to walk properly on a leash when he is still a puppy, or else he may pull and dash so much he hurts himself as an adult.

in the suburbs, where an owner may encounter a combination of grassy knolls and high-traffic areas. Some retractable leads even come with built-in dispensers for cleanup bags. My own dogs each have several conventional leashes, but without a doubt, it's their retractable leashes we use the most.

Collars also come in a variety of styles and materials. Again, cotton and nylon both work well, but the nylon tends to last a little longer. Even more important than the material, though, is the added feature of breakaway technology. Instead of a collar with a standard buckle-style closure, opt for one that clips together and breaks apart if it becomes caught on something. This simple feature could prevent your dog from being strangled if this ever happens to him.

A collar should fit snugly to prevent escape, but it should never be tight. To size your Springer for a collar, measure his neck. You should be able to slip two fingers comfortably beneath the tape. If you prefer to use a harness, measure the circumference of your Springer's chest just behind his front legs. Like collars, harnesses should lie close to the body, but they should never restrict movement or normal breathing.

Tags

When you register your dog with your local municipality, you will receive a numbered dog tag. When attached to your dog's collar, this item can help identify him if he ever becomes lost. To the average person on the street, however, this number alone means nothing. A better way to provide your dog with identification is to buy him a personalized tag.

Personalized tags are extremely inexpensive and easy to find. Many pet supply stores offer self-serve machines that engrave animal tags in just minutes while you wait. You can also order this custom-made item online. Be sure to include your dog's name, your address, and your phone number (including area code). And don't forget to attach the tag to your dog's collar. If he doesn't wear it, a tag is useless.

Toys

Most English Springer Spaniels love toys. The type your dog likes best will depend on his personality. Perhaps your Springer enjoys chasing balls or squeak toys. My female Spaniel, Molly,

About Head Harnesses

If your Springer puppy is easily distracted when walking on a leash, you may opt for a head harness instead of a conventional collar. Designed to wrap around your dog's muzzle, a head harness enables you to control the direction your Springer faces, effectively discouraging him from pulling. If he does pull, the very design of the harness pulls his head downward, also making it difficult for him to pull in any direction. If there is a downside to head harnesses, it is their close resemblance to muzzles. In some cases, this can make people a bit wary of approaching your dog (an impediment for socialization) and can be a little disconcerting for some owners, as well.

Provide plenty of toys for your Springer.

especially likes pigs and cows. Whenever we take her to the pet supply store, she will inevitably reach for one of these stuffed toys. Your dog might not be as specific in his likes and dislikes, but most do have preferences toward one type of toy or another.

If your dog is a chewer, reach for hardier items. Hard plastic toys work best for these Springers. Nylabone makes a fun line of toys for strong chewers. Molly also loves her Nylabone Brontosaurus, a flavored chew toy shaped like a dinosaur.

Interactive toys are perfect for providing your pet Springer with daily exercise. After all, any toy is more fun when a Springer has someone to throw it for him. Try a flying disc for a fun workout for both you and your pet right in your own backyard. Or give him an interactive toy when he must entertain himself for a while. Toys that distribute yummy treats when rolled just the right way are especially fun.

Beware of Vinyl

Beware of vinyl toys. Toxic chemicals called phthalates (pronounced THA-lates) are added to plastic to make it pliable. These also are what give vinyl its characteristic smell. The stronger a toy made from vinyl smells, the more phthalates it likely contains. The very property that makes phthalates so effective in softening plastic is the reason they are so dangerous: Phthalate molecules do not bond to the plastic, but rather move freely through it—into any surface with which it comes into contact, including your dog's skin and other tissue. They even release into the air, water, and earth.

In recent years, a great deal of scrutiny has focused on vinyl toys made for children. Research has shown that these additives interfere with the proper development of young people. Many state and federal governments around the world have even passed legislation restricting the use of phthalates in childcare items. In 2007, Governor Arnold Schwarzenegger signed a bill that banned the use of phthalates in children's products in California. Perhaps most compelling, though, is that the bulk of the research on phthalates has been conducted on animals. Dogs in particular are extremely vulnerable to the effects of phthalates, since their primary means of grasping an object is with their mouths.

Always check a toy's label before purchasing it. If you see the word "vinyl" or the acronym "PVC" (which stands for polyvinyl chloride), it means the toy contains phthalates. If a toy isn't clearly labeled, keep looking until you find a suitable item that you are certain doesn't contain one of these harmful ingredients.

With increasing awareness of the dangers of phthalates, some companies have begun labeling their vinyl pet toys "phthalate-free" or "nontoxic vinyl." Unfortunately, random testing of many products has determined that even toys bearing such claims do indeed contain these dangerous additives. There simply isn't such a thing as nontoxic vinyl. The only way to avoid phthalates is to avoid vinyl.

Impromptu Toys

Toys may also be found right on your kitchen counter. My own dogs regularly beg for empty paper towel tubes and plastic soda bottles. Think of the child at Christmas who has more fun playing with the empty box than her presents. To my dogs, getting a paper towel tube is a huge deal, probably because I only let them have this special treasure every once in a while (the downside to this makeshift toy is that it can make a big mess if your dog likes to shred it...as mine do). Picking up the pieces is more than worth it, though, when I see how much enjoyment this simple item offers them.

An empty soft drink bottle, on the other hand, makes no mess at all, but it can be extremely noisy when a dog chases it as it rolls across the floor. This is not an item to give your Springer if you have a headache. Also, be sure your dog doesn't puncture the plastic with his teeth or eat the cardboard from the paper towel tube. Both these "toys" require owner supervision.

MICROCHIPPING

If you have purchased a personalized identification tag for your English Springer Spaniel, you are off to great start at ensuring his safe return should he ever become lost. If your dog is ever stolen, though, a tag will do little to bring him back to you.

Microchipping your dog may be the only way to reunite with him if he ever becomes lost.

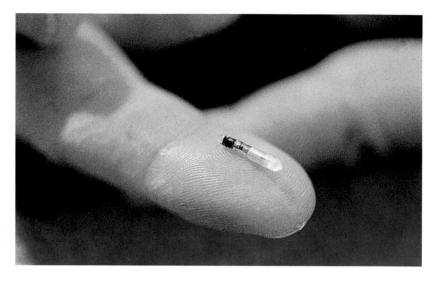

Your dog will barely feel the microchip being inserted into him.

Even a dimwitted thief will make it his top priority to remove your Springer's ID tag.

At one time, the most popular method of canine identification was tattooing. Many dog owners still go this route. Like a person's tattoo, a dog's tattoo is applied just under the animal's skin with a needle filled with special ink. Unlike a human, though, a dog must be anesthetized during this procedure. Another downside to this method is that a tattoo can be altered, rendering it far less useful.

Microchipping your Springer is a much more permanent and effective choice. A canine microchip, which is approximately the size of a grain of rice, can be inserted under your dog's skin (typically between his shoulder blades) with a needle during a routine veterinary visit, using absolutely no anesthesia. The process is no more painful than a vaccination. Your dog's unique number is then registered with the appropriate company. If your Springer becomes lost or stolen, a veterinarian or animal shelter worker can scan the chip to confirm his identity.

It is extremely important that you keep your contact information current with your microchip company. If you move or change your phone number, be sure to provide an update. Likewise, if you move far enough to switch to a different veterinarian, remember to let the new office staff know that your dog has been microchipped. Your Springer's chart should include this important number.

The AKC encourages owners to microchips their dogs. In certain areas, a microchip is even required by law if you own dog. In 1995, the city of Oakland, California became one of the first municipalities to draft an ordinance making it a crime not to microchip a canine companion.

As the practice of microchipping has become more and more popular, it has also become surprisingly affordable. Low-cost vaccination clinics, which are held at many pet supply stores, frequently offer microchipping at a reduced cost for pet owners. This can be especially helpful if you own more than one animal.

Few of us think it will ever happen to us, but the tragic reality is that one in three pets will become lost during his lifetime. Dogs are euthanized every day in shelters across this country simply because their owners haven't yet found them. Don't let your Springer be one of them.

Get the Picture

If your English Springer Spaniel is ever lost or stolen, the first thing you will need is an up-to-date photograph of your dog. As soon as possible, attach the photo to a piece of paper with your name and phone number written on it and make numerous

You have a better chance of being reunited with your lost dog if he is microchipped.

copies. Distribute the copies to as many people in your area as you can. Drop them off to all your neighbors. Ask any nearby schools and businesses if you may post these flyers in their windows. If people know what your Springer looks like, they will be much more likely to recognize him if they see him.

If your Springer has any distinguishing markings, be sure to capture them in your photograph. This will help others recognize him and also help you prove ownership once he is located. If your dog has been microchipped, it will be tough for a thief to claim him, but if he hasn't, this simple snapshot could help put the law on your side.

While your Springer is still a puppy, snap photos of him weekly to ensure that you have a current picture. Once he reaches adulthood, update the photo annually. Most importantly, don't procrastinate. Once your dog has become lost or stolen, it's too late.

WHEN THE OWNER'S AWAY

Choosing someone to care for your dog when you must be away from him can be a tough task. For most of us, our pets are like our children, and we want to make sure they are always in safe hands. Some people are fortunate enough to be able to bring their beloved pets to work with them—or to travel with them—but many cannot. And in some cases, staying home may even be better for your dog.

I struggled with this dilemma myself recently as my husband and I planned a family trip to Walt Disney World. At first, we considered driving from New England to Florida so that our two dogs wouldn't have to be left behind. Since one of our Spaniels suffers from epilepsy, we were especially concerned about being away from her for a full week. We even searched the web for hotels that allowed dogs and private rental homes in pet-friendly communities. Ultimately, though, we listened to our veterinarian, who recommended leaving both dogs in someone else's care. Since neither of our dogs had ever been on a road trip before, and since the stress of travel could possibly induce a seizure, our vet thought it would be better for us to leave our dogs in a more familiar environment.

Was this the right decision? I think so, but it was definitely a judgment call. Indeed, traveling can be an extremely upsetting event for many pet owners, whether they take their dogs along

Make the Right Choice

Be as selective in choosing a doggy daycare facility as you would be in selecting a daycare provider for your child. You must trust the staff at this facility with your beloved English Springer Spaniel. If you don't feel comfortable with the people or the accommodations, keep looking.

Traveling by Car

Dogs who enjoy car travel need not be confined to a carrier if your vehicle has an animal restraint harness. Most pet supply shops carry a wide range of doggy travel harnesses that buckle into most standard seat belts to secure your dog safely.

It is also a good idea to travel with your pet in the back seat of the car (although, never in the bed of a pick up truck!), because of the possibility of a front-seat passenger-side airbag deploying and causing possible harm to your pet in an accident.

Dogs should always be kept safely inside the car. Pets who are allowed to stick their heads out the window can be injured by particles of debris or become ill from having cold air forced into their lungs. Never transport a pet in the back of an open pickup truck.

Stop frequently to allow your pet to exercise and eliminate. Never permit your pet to leave the car without a collar, ID tag, and leash.

Never leave your pet unattended in a parked car. On warm days, the temperature in your car can rise to 120°F (49°C) in a matter of minutes, even with the windows opened slightly. Furthermore, an animal left alone in a car is an invitation to pet thieves.

(Courtesy of the Humane Society of the United States)

with them or not. Even owners who must leave their dogs while they work must decide whether to leave their dogs home alone or enroll them in a daycare program, the only other option for many people.

Doggy Daycare

Doggy daycare businesses have popped up in nearly every area of the country in recent years. Similar to daycare for human children, these companies keep canines safe and entertained while their owners are working. Even owners who work part-time (or not at all) can utilize daycare for its benefits of providing dogs with a little extra exercise and socialization.

Get a Recommendation

Choosing the right daycare facility may sound like a difficult task, but it doesn't have to be. Begin by asking fellow pet owners if they know any good doggy daycares in the area. Your dog's veterinarian should also be able to recommend a trustworthy business. Avoid thumbing through the phone book; word-of-mouth recommendations are usually much more reliable than selecting a daycare facility from an advertisement.

Your Springer must be current on all of his vaccinations if you plan to board him.

Once you have a particular place in mind, make a phone call to schedule a tour of the facility. Most businesses will welcome your visit.

What to Look For

The daycare should be clean and well maintained. A faint smell of bleach is often a good sign that things are being kept as sanitary as possible. Staff members should be friendly and possess an obvious love for dogs. Experience with training and veterinary medicine is a plus. Enough employees should be present to adequately handle the number of animals. A good ratio is one person for every ten dogs.

Ask Questions

Ask as many questions as you can during the tour. What types of activities are offered? How are squabbles between dogs handled? What if your dog gets hurt? A daycare should offer both active times and rest periods for all the animals. Timeout rooms for separating dogs who don't get along are a great idea. Physical punishments, though, should never be used. A licensed veterinarian does not have to be present at all times, but the daycare should have a plan for handling any medical emergencies that may arise.

The Application Process

If you decide you would like to enroll your dog in a daycare program, you must first fill out an application. If there is an opening, you and your English Springer Spaniel will be invited for an interview. All dogs must be evaluated to help ensure a safe environment for all animals involved. If your dog is accepted into a program, you will need to provide proof of all his immunizations. Each state has different laws about which vaccinations daycares must require. A daycare provider may also require additional shots that are not necessarily required by law. The specific requirements of each facility can vary from one facility to another, but nearly all providers require the Bordetella (or kennel cough) vaccine.

Turned Down From Daycare?

If your dog is not considered a good candidate for a daycare program, try not to take it personally. This doesn't mean that your dog is bad in any way. Not all dogs are well-suited to daycare. If you find yourself in this situation, consider hiring a pet sitter instead.

Pet Sitters

If you work an erratic schedule, or if you prefer that your dog remain in his own home when you are away, a pet sitter may be just the person for you. Working for an hourly or weekly fee, a pet sitter comes to your home to feed, walk, and play with your dog when you cannot. Some even stay overnight, as a house sitter would.

Interview a pet sitter as thoroughly as you would a daycare provider. In addition to trusting this person with your precious pet, you must also provide her with a key to your home, after all. Ask for references, and be sure to follow-up by checking them. Most importantly, listen to your instincts, and watch your dog's reactions to the person. If either you or your dog takes an instant disliking to a potential sitter, continue your search.

Boarding

Some dog owners choose to board their pets when they will be away for extended periods of time. Unlike daycare programs, boarding kennels offer pets modest accommodations when their owners are away overnight. Sometimes this means a crate; other facilities offer each boarder a larger, pen-sized area. You may board your pet for one night only or for several days and nights in a row, depending on the facility and your specific needs. The employees at a boarding service feed and walk the dogs several times each day, but they do not generally offer playtime activities or interactions with other animals.

Vaccinations

By law, boarding kennels must require the same vaccinations as daycare providers. This protects all the animals staying at the facility from certain illnesses that can be passed from one dog to another. It is especially important for dog owners to find a boarding kennel well in advance of actually needing boarding services. If your Springer needs to get any additional shots before his stay, you must have sufficient time to schedule the visit with your veterinarian. Also, because boarding kennels tend to fill up quickly during certain times of the year—around major holidays, for instance—you should also book your Springer's stay as early in advance as possible to ensure that there will indeed be a spot for him.

Search Around

You should use the same level of scrutiny when selecting a boarding kennel as you would for a daycare provider. Request a tour of the facilities, and make sure they are clean and well kept. Ask how many times each day your Springer will be walked and fed, and also ask how long each walk is. Getting outside to go to the bathroom often enough is important, but he should also be able to stretch his legs some, especially if he will be spending most of his time in a small space.

Toys of Your Own

Most boarding kennels allow owners to bring a few of their dogs' toys. Be sure you rub your hands over these items a few times before heading to the kennel, as your dog will be comforted by your scent during his time away from you. You should also bring enough food for your dog's stay.

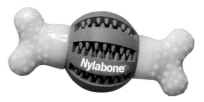

We'll be Back Soon

When the time comes to leave your pet, avoid long goodbyes. If your dog senses your own anxiety over leaving him through prolonged hugs and promises to return soon, he may have a more difficult time adjusting. If you make a point of staying positive, however, your attitude just might be contagious.

Chapter 4

FEEDING
Your English Springer Spaniel

One of the best ways to keep your English Springer Spaniel healthy is to feed him nutritious food each day. For some owners, this means selecting a quality prepackaged food; for others it involves cooking for their canine companions. Still other owners prefer feeding their Springers raw foods. Any of these diet plans can provide your dog with excellent nutrition, providing careful selections are made and serving sizes are kept moderate.

YOUR SPRINGER'S NUTRITIONAL NEEDS

Just like their owners, English Springer Spaniels have very specific nutritional needs, but these requirements differ significantly between humans and canines. For instance, in order to be healthy, people must eat fruits and vegetables rich in vitamin C, but dogs' bodies produce enough vitamin C on their own, so they do not need to eat foods containing it.

Carbohydrates

Carbohydrates (carbs) are organic compounds consisting of sugars, starches, and celluloses. Their primary function is to provide energy. Simple carbs are easily digested and absorbed, but complex varieties (starches) need more digestion, and therefore serve as a longer-lasting energy source. Common carbohydrates include cereal, pasta, rice, wheat, and vegetables. Like people, dogs need carbohydrates, but feeding the right kind is particularly important.

Fiber, another carbohydrate, serves many vital functions in your dog's gastrointestinal system—including helping to combat obesity by making a dog feel fuller after his meals. Fiber also helps prevent constipation. Since fiber slows the absorption of sugar, it can even be useful in managing diabetes.

Allergies may be a concern when dealing with carbohydrates, since carbs such as corn, wheat, and soy are common canine food allergens. Too much fiber can also have negative effects. In large quantities, it can prevent the absorption of vitamins and minerals, cause diarrhea and flatulence (gas), and increase both the volume and density of your dog's stools.

Your dog needs the proper balance of fats, protein, carbohydrates, and vitamins and minerals to grow up and become a happy and healthy adult.

Fats

While too much fat in any diet isn't desirable, dogs need fats, and they need considerably more fats than humans do. As the most concentrated source of dietary energy, fats help dogs maintain a healthy temperature, especially during cold weather. They also help keep a dog's skin healthy and make his coat shine. Essential fatty acids are necessary for maintaining normal immune and nervous systems. Finally, fats make food taste better. A food can only benefit your dog if he actually eats it.

No Simple Sugars

As in human diets, simple sugars are empty calories devoid of nutrients and should not be given to your English Springer Spaniel.

Protein

Dogs of all ages need protein. Composed of amino acids, protein is the most essential element in the diets of all animals. Puppies and geriatric dogs generally need even greater amounts of protein than do adult dogs. This is also the case for extremely active dogs. Foods rich in protein include meat, fish, eggs, dairy products, and legumes. Although vegetables and grains contain protein, these types of protein are more difficult for dogs to digest than those found in meats.

Vitamins and Minerals

Vitamins and minerals are necessary in every dog's diet for many purposes. Vitamins help maintain your dog's immune system so that it can fight off viral infections and other illnesses. They also aid in the proper absorption of fats and carbohydrates. There are two different kinds of vitamins—fat soluble and water soluble. If a dog is given too much of the former type, the excess will be stored within fatty tissue inside the body, leading to problems even worse than those from deficiencies. Water-soluble vitamins not used by your dog's body are passed out in his urine.

Trace minerals, such as iron and zinc, help prevent anemia, aid in cognitive functioning, and promote healthy coats. It is especially important, though, that vitamins and minerals are provided in very specific amounts and ratios. Minerals such as calcium and phosphorus, for instance, are needed for strong bones and teeth, but when unbalanced, they cannot be absorbed and utilized. Too much phosphorus in your dog's system can also lead to renal (kidney) disease.

Always provide your Springer with fresh, clean water. You can leave a few bowls around the house if you know he spends time in different areas throughout the day.

Water

Water is perhaps one of the most underrated dietary sources for good health in both animals and humans. Not only does your Springer need water to survive, he needs water to thrive. Water is the primary vehicle for transporting nutrients throughout your dog's body and for removing wastes from his system in the form of urine. It aids in digestion and circulation and is also responsible for regulating your dog's body temperature.

PREPACKAGED DOG FOODS

Take a quick stroll down the aisles of your local pet supply store, and you will see that deciding to feed a prepackaged food is only the beginning. A wide selection of types and brands exist. Does your Springer need a high energy formula, or would a dental-friendly formula be a smarter choice for him? Are the premium brands worth the higher price? Should you buy a dry kibble or a wet canned food?

Read the label of any food you consider buying to make sure it contains quality ingredients.

If your dog is extremely active, the higher amounts of protein and fat in a high-energy food will help him stay at the top of his game. Consider this type of formula if your Springer works in the field, competes in agility, or accompanies you while running or biking. Likewise, if your dog's teeth tend to accumulate plaque and tartar faster than you can keep up with brushing, consider the dental care variety. Many other specialty varieties are also available to match a long list of canine health and lifestyle needs.

Quality Ingredients

The most important thing is selecting a food made from nutritious ingredients. The first thing to look for is a sound protein source. At one time, the protein in most dog foods came primarily from beef and chicken byproducts—the parts of the animals deemed unfit for human consumption, such as hooves, beaks, and feet. This worked well for the dog food companies, because these cheap ingredients raised their profits right along with the foods' protein levels.

Although the U.S. Food and Drug Administration (FDA) still allows pet food companies to use these ingredients, more and more brands are choosing to eliminate byproducts from their foods. Instead they are offering foods made from human-grade lean meats, such as lamb, venison, and herring, in addition to more traditional choices like beef and chicken. You may find that one variety works better for your Springer than another, but all of these are sound protein sources.

Another ingredient to avoid is bone meal. Bone meal consists of ground animal bones and is another inexpensive way to boost protein content. The word "meal" can be tricky, though. While bone or byproduct meal is an undesirable ingredient, meat meal is an entirely different story. Meat meal is made by removing all water from a particular meat; the end result is a more concentrated source of protein. Meats contain an extremely high amount of water. Because dog food companies must list their ingredients in descending order on a food's label, this means a food whose first ingredient is lamb meal, for example, actually contains more lamb than if the first ingredient were lamb alone.

Two very common "filler" ingredients in many dog foods are

Fighting Food Allergies

If your Springer is allergic to the food he is eating, the first symptoms will be itching and other skin problems. An allergic dog may also suffer from ear infections or hair loss. Common food allergens for dogs include chicken, corn, soy, and wheat, but just like a person, a dog can experience an allergy to any type of food. While canine allergy testing procedures exist, these can be expensive and time-consuming. If you suspect your Springer is suffering from a food allergy, a more efficient approach is to ask your dog's veterinarian about placing your dog on a hypoallergenic diet. These prepackaged foods are available through most veterinary hospitals and consist exclusively of ingredients that pose a low risk of allergic reactions. (Some owners opt to cook hypoallergenic meals for their pets.) Once you have established your dog's new diet and his symptoms have been alleviated, you may then slowly reintroduce new foods one a time in hopes of identifying the offending ingredient or ingredients. At the very least, this will help you learn which foods your dog can tolerate.

Puppies must always have access to fresh water. Just remember to take him out regularly to empty his bladder.

corn and wheat gluten. In addition to offering little nutritional value, these ingredients are common food allergens. Chicken, while nutritious, is also known to trigger allergies in many dogs, particularly Spaniels. If your Springer eats a food containing one of these ingredients and starts scratching for no apparent reason, consider a diet change.

Preservatives

Kibble is usually the most cost-effective of prepackaged foods.

Always know the type of preservative that has been used to keep your Springer's food fresh. The Association of American Feed Control Officials (AAFCO) requires that this information appear on the package label. If you feed prepackaged foods, you will not be able to avoid preservatives, but some are much safer than others. Avoid foods preserved with synthetic preservatives such as butylated hydroxyanisole (BHA), butylated hydroxytoluene (BHT), and ethoxyquin. These have all come under particular scrutiny in recent years. Studies have shown that very high levels of BHA can cause tumors in the forestomachs of rats, mice, and hamsters. Since there has been no data collected relating to animals lacking a forestomach, and dog foods contain such a minute percentage (0.02 percent of the fat content only), the FDA currently allows the use of both these preservatives in dog foods. Although reliable data on ethoxyquin has been limited, there has been sufficient concern for the FDA to request that dog food companies lower the levels of ethoxyquin in their products. Presently, however, it is still allowed in dog foods at levels of up to 150 parts per million (ppm) or 0.015 percent.

The healthiest preservatives are called tocopherols. These vitamin-based preservatives are now used in many quality canine food brands. Unfortunately, foods that utilize tocopherols have shorter shelf lives, especially once a package has been opened. Rest assured, though, that your Springer should be able to consume the contents of a fairly large bag of dry kibble long before the expiration date on the package.

The Price of Quality

You definitely will pay more for quality food, but this is a worthwhile investment. You will also have to make a special trip to your local pet supply store for the best stuff, but again, this added effort offers many rewards. By feeding your dog nutritious food, you will lessen his risks for many diseases and very likely increase his lifespan. Bargain foods are anything but a good deal when you consider the costs to your Springer's health.

It is also important to remember that premium prices do not guarantee quality. Many high-priced brands contain many of the same inferior ingredients as lower-priced products. You must always read the package labels carefully.

Read the Labels

The wording alone on a dog food package can be misleading. By law, a pet food with the word "beef" in its name must contain at least 70 percent beef. If the phrasing is altered to "beef dinner," "beef platter," or "beef entrée," this requirement plummets to a mere 10 percent. If the term "with beef" is used, the food may contain as little as 3 percent beef.

The Perks of Parsley

Many dog owners garnish their pets' meals with fresh parsley as a means of preventing bad breath. Another way to utilize this herb's breath-freshening properties is by boiling it in water. Once the brew has cooled, just strain the leaves from the water, and pour the remaining liquid into ice cube trays before freezing. Add one cube to your Springer's water bowl daily for added taste and fresher breath.

The health benefits of feeding raw parsley may even outweigh the pleasant scent it leaves behind. High in vitamins A and C, raw parsley increases oxygen metabolism. It is also rich in calcium and iron. A single cup of minced parsley is filled with more beta-carotene, vitamin C, calcium, and iron than a large carrot, an orange, a cup of milk, and a full serving of liver combined!

Sizing up Kibble

If you feed your English Springer Spaniel kibble, be sure the pieces are the right size for him. Typically, puppy formulas are comprised of smaller food pieces made specifically for a pup's smaller mouth. Adult Springers, however, should have larger kibble. If the pieces are too small, they may not chew them sufficiently. This can cause some dogs to regurgitate, but even a dog who manages to keep his food down after gulping it may not be getting the most out of the nutrients. As your Springer ages, he may need to return to smaller food pieces. Senior dogs often have missing or decaying teeth, which can make chewing up larger pieces difficult and even painful.

Some companies have also found an insidious way of making their products appear more nutritious than they are. Since ingredients lists must be arranged in descending order according to weight, some manufacturers split ingredients into various subcategories. Rice and rice gluten, for example, may be listed separately—far below chicken—when in fact these ingredients together far outweigh the amount of meat in the food. When it comes to nutrition, dog owners must always stay on their toes.

Dry Food (Kibble)

Dry food, or kibble, is the most popular choice of dog owners who feed prepackaged food to their pets. Kibble is typically the most economical food choice. It is extremely convenient, too. Virtually no preparation is required, and it can be left in your dog's bowl all day without spoiling. It is also easy to transport to doggy daycare or on vacation.

Kibble is frequently praised for being better for a dog's teeth than softer foods. While this is true, it is important not to infer too much from this claim. All foods when mixed with saliva can lead to plaque and tartar if canine oral care is skimped. Therefore, dogs eating all types of food must have their teeth brushed regularly.

If you opt to feed your Springer dry food, purchase an airtight container for storage. A bag should never be merely rolled or clipped closed. Exposure to even a small amount of air puts food on the fast-track to spoilage. Air can also cause a healthy food to lose many of its vitamins and minerals. When transferring food from its bag to a new container, always keep the package label. This can come in handy if you need to consult the information at a later time—especially in the event of a recall.

When refilling your dog's kibble container, be sure to wait until all the food from the previous bag has been removed. Never combine new kibble with old, as the older pieces will spoil before the new pieces. Also, wash the container thoroughly each time you add new food. If you skip this important step, crumbs left at the bottom can become rancid and contaminate your dog's kibble.

Canned Food

Canned food has a longer shelf life than dry food. Like dry food, though, this wet food must be stored carefully once it has been opened. Always keep leftovers in a sealed container in your refrigerator until your dog's next meal—and discard any food that remains after a day or two. Plastic covers made specifically to fit these cans work great in the interim.

Many dogs enjoy the added aromas that wet food offers. Owners can even enhance this satisfying smell by heating wet food before serving it. If you feed dry food and want to do the same thing, just add a little water to your dog's kibble before heating it. Use caution when heating food in microwave ovens, though, as either type of food can become extremely hot in just a matter of seconds. Placing your finger in the center of your Springer's bowl before offering it to him should give you a good idea of whether the food's temperature is safe for your pet.

Canned food can be a highly nutritious and convenient choice. Because of its airtight design, canned food doesn't need the same preservatives as dry food to protect it from oxidation (spoilage). You may buy as little or as much as you like. You will need to brush your Springer's teeth more often if you go the wet route, though. Daily brushing is a must with this type of food.

Do not reward begging. This only encourages your Springer to continue this habit.

Semi-Moist

Some foods offer a compromise between the benefits of dry food and the appeal of wet food. The most nutritious of these semi-moist foods are called dog food rolls. These foods, which are packaged similar to salamis, are becoming increasingly popular with dog owners. As with all other types of dog food, however, careful scrutiny is a must when selecting a brand. The food you choose should meet all the same requirements as kibble or canned food.

Like all types of dog food, the least nutritious semi-moist foods are those sold in supermarkets and discount stores. These foods are frequently packaged in easy-to-feed individual portions and contain a massive amount of preservatives and other artificial ingredients, as well as added salt and sugar. Your Springer may gobble up these semi-moist meals if given the chance, but they are the canine equivalent to human fast food: an exorbitant amount of empty calories.

HOMECOOKING

One of the best ways to know exactly what your English Springer Spaniel is eating is to cook fresh foods for him. Although this type of feeding regimen may seem like it would be extremely time-consuming and expensive, this doesn't have to be the case. Many owners who practice homecooking for their pets integrate making meals for their dogs into their own culinary routines.

Is ground turkey on sale this week? Pick up a little extra for your Springer. Buying carrots for coleslaw? Grind one up to sprinkle over that turkey. Although carrots are often recommended as a healthy teeth-cleaning treat, carrots and many other vegetables retain their best nutritional qualities when ground into tiny pieces for pets. Dogs tend to chew their food only minimally and swallow it before important enzymes can be released. This doesn't mean you can't feed your dog carrot sticks from time to time, though. One of the benefits of homecooking is the delightful variety it offers pets.

Many veterinarians suggest placing dogs on homecooked diets at least temporarily to help relieve bouts of diarrhea or constipation. (Incidentally, canned pumpkin works great for either problem. Just be sure to grab the pure pumpkin from the

Consider Homecooking

The heat and pressure used in the manufacturing process diminishes many vitamins and minerals in prepackaged dog foods. Homecooking is a smart way to reclaim many of these nutrients for your dog. If you regularly prepare meals for yourself and your human family members, you will likely find that numerous foods that are good for you are also healthy for your Springer.

grocery store shelf and not the pie filling, which is loaded with sugar.) Homecooking is also frequently recommended for dogs suffering from various medical conditions, such as allergies or gastrointestinal problems. It has been suggested that this feeding method can even help dogs with more serious problems, like epilepsy and kidney disease. Many owners have consequently drawn the conclusion that if feeding homecooked foods is good for a sick dog, there must be advantages to cooking for healthy pets, too.

Balance

One of the clearest benefits to homecooking is balance, but this can only be achieved through careful planning and intentional variety. If you would like to cook for your Springer, talk to your vet. She can help you decide how much protein and which vegetables, for example, to include in your pet's menus. She may even be able to suggest a good cookbook of recipes written specifically for dogs. Even healthy foods should always be offered in moderation. Likewise, if you overlook an important nutrient, many of the advantages of homecooking can be lost to this deficiency.

Springers will eat everything that is available to them, so it is best not to free-feed them. Doing so can lead to obesity.

Two Foods to Use in Moderation

Carbohydrates and fruits are two types of food for concern here. The benefits and liabilities of carbohydrates are often debated among nutritionists. Dogs do not require high amounts of carbs in their diets—too many can even be detrimental—but carbohydrates do have some redeeming qualities. Carbs provide long-lasting energy, and they assist in the digestion of other foods.

An excellent carbohydrate to include in your Springer's diet is cooked oatmeal. Skip the sugar and fancy flavorings, though. Fruits, while nutritious, come with an excess of natural sugar. They can still be offered from time to time, but veggies are highly preferable.

The Staples

The staples of a healthy canine diet include lean meats and vegetables rich in vitamins A, B, D, E, and K. Because they contain protein, meats are important for the growth and repair of body tissue. Dairy products can be problematic for Springers, since most dogs are lactose intolerant. Plain yogurt and cottage cheese, however, are the most common exceptions and great ways to offer your dog calcium. Fats also play an important role in the canine diet. In addition to providing warmth, fats also assist a dog's body in the absorption of vitamin D.

Time

While many English Springer Spaniel owners fit homecooking into their schedules, the downside of this regimen is the undeniable time commitment required. The legwork alone involved in learning exactly which nutrients your Springer needs (and which he doesn't) can be considerable. Additionally, you will need to spend added time brushing your dog's teeth if he is eating regular cooked meals.

If all this sounds like too much for you to juggle, consider utilizing homecooking as a means of supplementing your dog's commercial diet. Grind those carrots over kibble instead of turkey, or add a little strip steak to your dog's dinner one night each week. If you are certain you want to cook for your pet, consider using the prepackaged food as the supplement to ensure that you have all your nutritional bases covered. Use whatever combination you and your vet decide is best for you and your Springer as you learn all that you can about cooking for your pet.

RAW FOODS

Many dog owners and veterinarians recommend feeding raw diets. Known by the acronym BARF (which stands for "bones and raw food" or "biologically appropriate raw food"), this regimen is based on the fact that most foods retain even more of their nutrients when they are served uncooked. Proponents of raw feeding plans point out that domesticated dogs evolved from wolves, after all, and a wolf's diet consists exclusively of raw foods. Many raw-feeding owners also insist that their dogs' excellent health, shiny coats, and increased energy levels are all evidence that this type of diet is ideal.

Raw diets typically include a variety of foods, including beef, chicken, and eggs. Vegetables are also an important part of this feeding regimen, as are a limited number of fruits and carbohydrates. If your dog tolerates dairy, cheese can also be fed. Owners may choose to prepare raw foods for their pets personally (many foods must be chopped or ground before serving) or to purchase prepackaged raw meals that can be frozen.

Research the diet that interests you thoroughly before committing your dog to it. There are both supporters and critics of vegetarian, vegan, and raw food diets.

If you are having trouble getting your Springer to eat his vegetables, try offering them before any meats. (Lima beans will always pale in comparison to sirloin in your Springer's eyes.) Also, be sure your dog is hungry when you feed him.

Critics, however, warn that the risks associated with feeding raw foods vastly outweigh the rewards. While they are great for a dog's teeth, bones can be a significant choking hazard. They can also cause life-threatening intestinal obstructions. Bacteria such as *Escherichia coli* (commonly called *E. coli*) and *Salmonella* are also very real dangers, even for a dog's seemingly cast-iron stomach. Raw meats can also contain harmful parasites. Even freezing

Healthy Appetites

English Springer Spaniels delight in eating. Unlike many other dog breeds, whose appetites tend to wane as they get older, most Springers will readily lick their food bowls clean well into their golden years without any coaxing. In fact, many Springer breeders warn that a poor appetite at any age is cause for concern. It could be a symptom of a health problem, such as an abscessed tooth or gum inflammation—or even a more serious condition, such as kidney or liver disease.

the meat does not necessarily eliminate the presence of these microorganisms.

VEGETARIAN DIETS

Some owners prefer not to feed their dogs any meat at all. Instead, they feed only vegetables and in some cases dairy. Some will go a step further and offer a completely vegan diet. Vegetarian regimens may contain eggs, for instance, but vegan diets are completely free of all foods derived from animals. These include dairy products. (Most vegans also abstain from using other products made from animals, such as leather shoes for themselves and leather leashes for their pets.)

Canine vegetarianism is a controversial issue. Numerous breeders warn against feeding a Springer an exclusively vegetarian diet. Dogs need a high amount of protein in the foods they eat. While protein is found in certain veggies, it can often be difficult for a dog to digest in vegetable form. Soy, a common protein source in both human and canine vegetarian diets, is also a common allergen in dogs.

Dogs also need two amino acids: L-carnitine and taurine. If you wish to feed your Springer a vegetarian or vegan diet, look for a product containing both of these important nutrients. Deficiencies of these amino acids have been linked to dilated cardiomyopathy, a serious cardiovascular disease that causes a dog's heart to become overly large and ultimately nonfunctional. Supplemental forms of L-carnitine and taurine can also be purchased at most health food stores. These are must-have ingredients for an owner feeding a homecooked vegetarian or vegan diet.

FEEDING THROUGH THE AGES

As English Springer Spaniels grow and mature, their dietary needs also change. How much and how often you feed your dog aren't the only considerations. The specific ratios of certain nutrients should also be adjusted as puppies move into adulthood and adult dogs become seniors. By staying on top of your dog's changing dietary requirements, you will help him move into each new phase of his life with optimum health and vigor.

Your Springer's diet will change as he ages.

Feeding a Springer Puppy

Proper growth is highly dependent on a Springer puppy's diet. Because puppies need higher amounts of protein and fat than do adult dogs, owners should opt for a puppy formula when selecting a prepackaged food for these younger dogs. Once your Springer has reached between 80 and 90 percent of his adult weight—typically around six months of age, he should then be transitioned to an adult formula.

You may feed your Springer puppy two to three times a day. More important than how often you offer his meals, though, is that you establish a consistent feeding schedule for your new pet. Most English Springer Spaniel puppies will eat as much food as they are given, so leaving food available at all times (also called free feeding) can quickly lead to obesity. If you wish to practice free feeding, wait until your Springer is at least a year old so that he has at least had a chance to establish a healthy eating routine. Even adult dogs often have a hard time maintaining a healthy weight on a free-feeding plan.

Most prepackaged foods offer a suggested serving amount right on the package. If your puppy is gaining weight too quickly or too slowly, however, an adjustment may be necessary. You can also consult your dog's veterinarian for feeding advice.

Feeding an Adult Springer

Even if your adult Springer will be eating the same brand of food as he did as a puppy, he can experience stomach upset if the switch to the adult variety is made too abruptly. Any dietary changes should be made gradually for this reason. Begin by replacing only about 25 percent of your Springer's puppy food with his new adult fare. With each passing week, this percentage can then be increased by another 25 percent until your dog has completely transitioned to the new food.

If you fed your Springer puppy three meals a day, eliminate his mid-day meal when he makes the leap to adult food. Adult Springers are usually excellent eaters. If your dog proves to be an exception, first consider the amount of exercise he is getting. Often, all that is needed to stimulate a Springer's appetite is a slight increase in activity. If this doesn't do the trick, consult your veterinarian.

Sample Feeding Schedule for Each Phase of Life

PUPPIES LESS THAN SIX MONTHS	PUPPIES BETWEEN SIX MONTHS AND ONE YEAR	ADULT DOGS	SENIOR DOGS
Feed your English Springer Spaniel puppy three times each day — in the morning, midday, and in the early evening. Be sure to offer water with each meal, but remove it one to two hours before bedtime.	When your Springer makes the change to adult food around six months of age, eliminate his midday meal. Fresh water should be made available at all times once housetraining success is achieved.	Feed adult Springers twice daily. Keep an eye on the scale, and if necessary, adjust your dog's food intake to keep his weight within an acceptable range. If your dog is extremely active, a high-energy formula may be necessary.	As your Springer enters his golden years, consider feeding him soft foods to make his meals more appealing and easier on his teeth. A senior formula rich in protein and lower in calories should be introduced around the age of seven or eight.

A Weighty Issue

The best way to tell if your English Springer Spaniel is overweight is by placing him on a scale. Males should weigh approximately 50 pounds (23 kg), with females weighing in at just a little less—about 45 pounds (20 kg). A more hands-on approach is to simply feel your dog's chest for his ribs. They should be discernible but not prominent. If you have to press deeply, your Springer is probably overweight.

A little extra weight may seem inconsequential, but just an extra 5 pounds (2.3 kg) can lead to health problems in this breed. Overweight Springers are more prone to diabetes and heart disease, as well as to joint problems like hip and elbow dysplasia. Dogs carrying extra weight are also more likely to tear ligaments or otherwise injure themselves when running and jumping.

Additional changes to your Springer's diet may be necessary as he moves through adulthood. Your dog's weight is usually a superb barometer for nutrition. If your dog is eating nutritious food and maintaining a healthy weight, no changes should be necessary. If, however, your dog is gaining weight, it may be time to place him on a weight-loss formula until he sheds the extra pounds. Likewise, a medical condition may make a dietary change (either a temporary or a permanent one) necessary.

Feeding an Older Springer Spaniel

Once your English Springer Spaniel enters the final third of his life—around the age of seven or eight—he should begin eating food made especially for senior dogs. Just like a human's, a dog's metabolism slows with age. Therefore, older Springers typically need fewer calories and less fat than do adult dogs. Older dogs also need more protein, since their ability to metabolize this nutrient appears to lessen with age. Healthy senior Springers may require as much as 50 percent more protein than younger adult dogs. Because problems such as arthritis and other joint problems often accompany old age, senior diets containing supplements such as glucosamine may also be helpful.

Some dogs experience decreased senses of smell and taste at they age. This can result in a decreased appetite. To combat this problem, try adding a tablespoon of canned dog food or chicken broth to your pet's dry food. Heating food can also help release appealing aromas. If your dog has missing or decaying teeth (another reason for a waning appetite), consider swapping him from kibble to wet food to make eating a more comfortable experience. You should also schedule a professional dental cleaning with your dog's vet. Any broken or diseased teeth should be removed at this time.

SUPPLEMENTATION AND SPECIAL DIETS

The best source for the nutrients your dog's body needs is the food he eats. Think omega-3 fatty acids will help your Springer's coat look first rate? Consider adding some cooked salmon to his kibble a couple times a week. Want to boost your dog's immune system with some beta-carotene? Sweet potatoes are full of it; bake one and split it with your dog for a tasty and healthy treat.

Slowly incorporating exercise into an overweight Springer's life will help him lose weight. Doing too much too soon, though, can lead to injury.

If your dog suffers from a health problem, supplementing his diet with certain vitamins or minerals may be necessary.

Selenium, for example, is beneficial to animals suffering from cancer or inflammatory bowel disease. Vitamin E is also used to help canine cancer patients, as well as dogs suffering from heart disease. Even when supplements are clearly indicated, however, owners must be extremely careful in offering them. Dosages must be based on an individual dog's size, age, and overall health. Many supplements (like selenium) can be toxic when administered in overly high doses.

Prescription diets are also available for pets with certain medical conditions. Dogs suffering from kidney disease, for instance, require a diet low in both protein and phosphorus. Each regimen contains the specific nutrients that best help animals with that particular health affliction. These diets are sold exclusively at veterinarian's offices, and like prescription medications, they require a vet's authorization.

FEEDING AND EATING PROBLEMS

Feeding your Springer a sensible amount of healthy food can help him live a long, happy life. Overfeeding (in either food quantity or calories), however, can lead to a myriad of health problems for your beloved pet. It is also important to teach your Springer good manners when it comes to eating. By establishing healthy eating routines early, you lay the foundation for food to become your dog's friend, not his foe.

Obesity

Because this breed has such a fondness for food, obesity can quickly become a problem if owners don't keep a watchful eye on their Springers' food intake. Serious illnesses such as diabetes, heart disease, and joint problems are the sad side effects to your dog's eating food too high in fat and calories. It is important to remember that even healthy foods must be served in moderation. If your dog is eating more calories than he is burning each day—whether they are coming from french fries or carrot sticks, he will gain weight. And like people, dogs tend to put weight on much more quickly than they can take it off.

If your Springer is overweight, talk to your veterinarian about the best approach to remedy the situation. The two most obvious means of lowering that number on the scale are diet and exercise. You may need to approach the latter strategy

Sneaking in Exercise With Treats

If you are watching your Springer's weight, consider offering him his edible treats inside puzzle-style toys. These fun toys that dispense treats when maneuvered in just the right way offer a dual purpose. First, they get your dog moving, an essential component to keeping his weight under control. Second, they stimulate his brain. The mental challenge these toys provide help keep your dog's mind as fit as his body.

Remember to give edible treats only as rewards. Create a new habit of making exercise a prerequisite to your dog's morning biscuit. And increase the impact by swapping that fatty biscuit for a healthier treat. Fresh veggies are a great choice, but organic dog biscuits are also available.

Exercise shouldn't always be followed by food, of course, but linking the treats you do offer your dog with physical activity will help keep extra pounds at bay. Praise, on the other hand, can be given freely. All the *good boys* in the world won't cause your Springer to gain a single ounce.

carefully, though, if your dog is obese or if he already suffers from a health problem. Exercise can be a bit of a conundrum for a severely overweight animal. You must increase your pet's activity level in order to increase his metabolism, but the extra weight he is carrying places him at an increased risk of injury.

Changes should always be made slowly. First, your vet may recommend transitioning your pet to a weight-control diet. A smart strategy is to also add exercise to your Springer's routine gradually. If your long-term goal is to run a mile with your dog each day, for example, you may start by walking about half this distance for the first week. As your pet's tolerance increases, you may then lengthen the walk or pick up the pace a bit.

Follow your vet's orders carefully, especially if your Springer suffers from a medical condition. Exercise should always be a positive addition to your pet's routine. It should never exacerbate a health problem.

In extreme situations of obesity, a veterinarian may suggest

Don't overfeed your dog, no matter how hungry you think he is.

placing a dog on a prescription diet for weight loss. Yes, even diet pills are now available for dogs. A canine drug called dirlotapide works much the same as a human appetite suppressant. Since it minimizes hunger and prevents your dog's body from absorbing fat, dirlotapide is very effective. Still, both prescription diets and diet pills should only be used in extreme cases and for short periods of time.

As your Springer begins losing his extra weight, movement should become easier for him, and his endurance should increase as well. Still, continue to make changes slowly. If you think your dog is ready for running, begin by walking, a great warm-up for even the fittest dog. You may then jog together for a short distance before returning to walking, a necessary cool-down period, toward the end of your workout.

Jogging is far from your only choice when it comes to increasing your Springer's exercise level. If you and your dog enjoy visiting the beach, make swimming a part of his exercise routine. Bringing a ball or flying disc for him to chase can make all that movement even more fun for both you and your pet. Be creative. In the summer, our dog Molly jumps through the sprinkler with our son in our backyard. My husband and I regularly bring both our dogs to a set of public tennis courts close to our home. This enclosed area is perfect for playing fetch.

Owners can also include their dogs in their own exercise routines. Many Springers love running alongside their favorite humans while they rollerblade or bike. Our dogs enjoy chasing soccer balls with our son while he practices his all-time favorite sport.

If you do not offer your Springer food from the table, he will not expect a treat every time you sit down to eat.

Your Springer will love the outdoors as much as you do.

What the dog is doing is far less important than the movement itself. By making physical activity an ongoing priority, owners can help their dogs avoid the problems caused by obesity.

Excess/Wrong Treats

All dog owners enjoy treating their pets occasionally. My dogs know whenever we go to the pet supply store for dog food that they will each also get a special cookie from the canine snack buffet before heading home. I have even been known to share a bit of my favorite white cheddar popcorn with my precious pets once in a while. The key to healthy treating is being smart about what kinds of treats are offered and how often they are given.

Junk food isn't good for people or pets, but it can be especially dangerous for dogs. Chocolate, for example, contains an alkaloid called theobromine. Because dogs cannot process this alkaloid as quickly as people can, consuming chocolate can adversely affect a dog's heart, kidneys, and central nervous system. Theobromine poisoning can even be fatal.

Treats need not be poisonous, however, to be poor choices for pets. Foods high in fat or sugar should also be avoided. Fortunately, most Springers are as content with fresh fruits and vegetables as they are with cupcakes and potato chips. In addition to causing your dog to gain unnecessary weight, these latter foods can also lead to chronic conditions like heart disease and diabetes.

Offering treats too often can also be a problem. Even snacks made specifically for dogs can contain excessive amounts of fat and calories. A great way to avoid over-treating without having to reward your dog less often is breaking larger dog biscuits into two or more pieces to make smaller serving sizes.

Finally, remember that a treat doesn't have to be edible. As much as most Springers adore food, they also delight in spending time with their favorite people. Taking your dog for a walk or a fun play session at the park is a great way to treat both his body and spirit.

Manners

Many dog owners forget about teaching their pets good food manners until unpleasant behaviors like begging develop. In this situation, prevention is preferable to correction. From the day your Springer joins your family, refrain from feeding him directly from the table. Also, do not react to begging by giving in to your dog's pleas. If you follow these two simple rules, begging should never become a problem. Once you reward this undesirable behavior with food, however, your dog will be much more likely to continue begging. After all, he has now been shown that it works.

If your dog has already begun begging for food when you eat, the most important step is remaining steadfast in your unwillingness to offer him a taste of whatever you are eating. Next, if he still persists when you don't acquiesce, remove him from the room. You may allow him to re-enter at a later time, but if he goes back to begging, remove him again until you have finished your meal. Repeat this process as often as necessary.

Some owners find it helpful to feed their Springers before the family's meal times. Others find it necessary to remove their dogs from the room each time they eat. Although the breed is not the most notorious for drooling, Springers can produce enough extra saliva to make a person with a weak stomach lose interest in eating. If the slobber bothers you, simply crate your dog or place him in another room during family meal times. There will be many other activities the two of you can share.

And speaking of sharing, it is important to understand that it is not the sharing of food that leads to begging. If you wish to give your dog a small portion of what you are eating, simply place that portion in his bowl at your kitchen counter. In this way, he understands that his food is his, and your food is yours. If he sees you take food from your plate and offer it to him, he will quickly see your plate as his domain and start demanding his share at each meal.

Remember, barking

and fussing are not the only ways dogs beg. Sitting and staring are also forms of this behavior. If your dog begs in this more subdued fashion, follow the same technique described here until the behavior stops.

FOOD DESIRE AS PRIMARY TRAINING OPPORTUNITY

Like people, dogs tend to work harder when rewards are involved. Edible rewards in particular are extremely effective in teaching dogs new tricks. For the result to be a lasting one, however, some adjustments will be necessary as your dog masters each task he is taught.

Whenever you begin teaching a new command, start by using a healthy, bite-sized treat as a reward. Soft dog treats, cubed chicken or cheese, or another food your Springer especially likes should work well. You may even purchase treats made specifically for training purposes. Avoid crunchy items or foods that require a lot of chewing, as both can distract your dog from the training process. Also, train your Springer before a meal rather than afterwards. A little hunger can equal a lot of motivation.

In the beginning, praise and food rewards should be given simultaneously each and every time your dog performs a specific command. (Initially, you may even reward him for performing only part of the task at hand.) Once he is complying with the command most of the time, you should then start giving the edible rewards only intermittently. Eventually, food rewards should only be given occasionally to maintain the desired behavior, but continue to praise your Springer consistently whenever he follows the command.

Even with its clear advantages, using food as a reward can certainly have its downside. Owners must remain vigilant of their dogs' weight and overall health. If calories are a concern, consider using a small portion of your Springer's dog food for the day as rewards during training, instead of adding to his daily food intake with treats. Some owners prefer not to use food as a reward at all. If you are successful in training your dog without food rewards, there is no reason you must add it to your training program.

C h a p t e r

5

GROOMING
Your English Springer Spaniel

A t first glance, grooming an English Springer Spaniel may seem pretty labor intensive. The feathered coat of a show-quality Springer can look like it took days to brush, bathe, and comb into place. Fortunately, caring for this breed's appearance isn't nearly as difficult as it seems. By spending just a few minutes each day performing small jobs, owners can make grooming time a quick—and even enjoyable—chore for all involved.

START WHILE YOUR SPRINGER IS YOUNG

To make grooming a trouble-free task, start early and remain consistent. Beginning the day you bring your Springer puppy home, pick him up several times each day and place him gently on his grooming table. You needn't actually brush him each time you set him on the table. Your initial goal is to simply get him comfortable with standing on this surface. Holding onto him carefully, let him move his paws around so that he understands that flailing about will only cause him to lose his footing. Reward him for tolerating this exercise.

Some owners are tempted to postpone grooming until a dog has had a chance to settle in to his new environment. Don't make this mistake. Putting off important tasks like brushing and nail trimming will only allow your Springer to settle into a schedule that doesn't include these necessary parts of pet care. Show your puppy right away that grooming feels good, and you will ease any fears he may have. Your dog may never truly love bath time—although many Springers do—but he will be much easier to handle if he accepts grooming time as part of his regular routine.

GROOMING—A PROACTIVE APPROACH TO GOOD HEALTH

Regular grooming not only keeps your dog looking and feeling his best, but it can also help keep him healthy. Often, an owner can discover early signs of illness while grooming. If your Springer's normally lustrous coat looks dull or you notice dry, rough, or bald patches when brushing him, talk to your veterinarian. The problem

Table Talk

Many English Springer Spaniel owners consider a grooming table to be a must-have item. As someone who has groomed in nearly every setting imaginable, I can tell you that tables offer numerous advantages. Using a table makes grooming considerably easier on your back. Grooming tables also come with safety harnesses to help keep pets in place and nonskid surfaces to prevent slipping. Most fold for easy storage, making them highly portable—a perk for owners who show their Springers in conformation.

With all their benefits, though, grooming tables are not right for everyone. Some owners prefer grooming their pets on the floor. If your dog will stand for grooming in a less restrictive area like this, and your back can handle it, there is no reason you must add a grooming table to your shopping list. One of my favorite places to groom my own dogs is outdoors in the grass. They seem to tolerate the process a little better in the fresh air and sunshine.

If you choose to groom your dog in a more unconventional area like outdoors, be sure to take all proper safety precautions. If your backyard is not fenced, keep your Springer leashed at all times. If you place your dog on a piece of furniture, make sure it isn't so high off the ground that your dog could get hurt by jumping off it. A great trick I have discovered to make floors less slippery is setting my dogs on a rubber-backed throw rug or bathmat while grooming them. This simple item also helps differentiate grooming time from play time. When my dogs see me spread out my green throw rug, they know it's time to get pretty.

could be a parasite, a thyroid disorder, or even poor nutrition. By uncovering the problem early, you increase the chances of correcting it before it can become a more serious issue.

Responses to Your Touch

The more time you spend grooming your dog, the more you will learn about the way he responds to the various tasks. Perhaps your Springer always struggles during nail trims, or maybe he has a particular dislike for having his ears cleaned. If your dog cries or yelps when you touch him, though, he is probably sick or injured. An infection, for instance, can make a dog's ears extremely sensitive to touch. Sprains and bone fractures can also be especially painful. Dogs are generally very resilient animals. If your Springer pulls away from you with great urgency, this is a sign that something is wrong.

Look Closely

Not all illnesses present themselves so blatantly, though. Sometimes owners must examine their dogs more closely for signs of a problem. Dogs have retained a strong survival instinct from their wild ancestry, and this can cause them to hide many signs of illness from us. Wild dogs often shun sick pack members. For this reason, many dogs suffering from an illness will do their best to hide their pain.

Lumps and Bumps

No matter how hard he tries, however, a dog cannot hide suspicious-looking lumps and bumps. These are among the scariest symptoms of illness an owner may discover while grooming. Thankfully, finding them as early as possible can help identify them as malignant or benign. Even if a growth proves to be cancerous, early detection improves a dog's chance of survival—thus making vigilant grooming an invaluable means of maintaining good health.

BRUSHING

Because of their long coats, English Springer Spaniels in full coat should be brushed daily. Field dogs are often trimmed shorter than show dogs. If you prefer to keep your dog in a shorter pet clip like this, you may brush your Springer's fur only once or twice per week instead. Even if you send your dog to a professional for more intricate grooming, though, you will still need to brush him at home regularly.

Grooming is the perfect time to inspect your dog for scratches, stings, or other marks requiring your immediate attention.

Remember, brushing does far more than simply keep tangles at bay. Brushing removes dead hair from your Springer's coat. English Springer Spaniels are notorious shedders, so regular brushing will help reduce the amount of hair that makes its way to your clothing and carpeting. Brushing also removes dirt and other debris from your pet's coat. The more often you brush, the less often you will have to bathe your Springer.

Do I Need Professional Help?

If you are too busy to perform all your dog's grooming tasks personally, employing a professional groomer can be a lifesaver. It may be easy to find time for simpler tasks like brushing, but bathing an English Springer Spaniel can be a big production. Groomers are also ideal for owners who are intimidated by tasks such as trimming their dogs' toenails. On the other hand, if you would like to learn more about the grooming process, going the do-it-yourself route is a great way to save some money while spending some extra time with your pet.

Always brush your dog before bathing him. Any hair that has become snarled or matted will be virtually impossible to disentangle once water is added to the equation. Parts of the body most prone to matting are the belly and the backside of the legs.

Brushing Supplies

The type of brush you buy can make a big difference in how easy it is to keep your dog clean and comfortable. This breed has a double coat. Soft-bristled brushes may keep the surface of your Springer's coat looking good, but they usually don't reach the skin—a must for effective brushing. Slicker brushes, on the other hand, do a great job of reaching the skin. They can scratch your dog and damage his coat, though. This can be of particular importance if your dog has sensitive skin or you show him in conformation. Pin-style brushes are usually ideal for brushing this breed.

All English Springer Spaniel owners also need two different types of combs: a medium-tooth comb and a flea comb. When used after brushing, the former tool will help identify any tiny knots you may have missed when brushing your pet. The latter is the only tool that will reliably tell you if any fleas are hiding in your Springer's abundant coat. Although plastic versions of both types work equally well, I prefer metal for the simple reason that this material is virtually indestructible.

If your Springer's hair is prone to tangles, consider investing in a mat splitter. This sickle-shaped tool can cut the most menacing knots from your dog's coat when you think disentangling them would be too time-consuming or painful for your pet. Be especially careful when using this item, though: it's effective because it holds a razor blade.

How to Brush Your Springer Spaniel

Begin each brushing session by simply running your fingers over your Springer's coat. If your dog enjoys being massaged, as most dogs do, this will help make the experience a fun and relaxing one for him. It also gives you a chance to check for any abnormalities in his coat.

Many groomers recommend misting a dog with a grooming or detangling spray prior to brushing. When used in

All dogs require regular grooming, from show dogs to couch buddies.

moderation, these products help prevent hair breakage and can make it easier to brush through mat-prone areas. Many also come in pleasing scents. If you use too much, however, the dampness will tighten any knots that are present.

Once you're ready to get down to business, begin by brushing your dog's head and ears. From there, move to his back, legs, chest, and belly. To remove as much dead hair as possible, brush against the hair growth first, and then brush with it. Be sure to reach the skin, but be careful not to scratch it.

Power Tools

If you will be showing your Springer in conformation, you will likely use a number of different brushes and other tools to keep his coat looking its very best. A wide variety of grooming gear is available just for brushing alone. As one English Springer Spaniel breeder told me, grooming can make the difference between placing first or not at all.

Praise your dog throughout this process. If you offer your Springer edible rewards, like Nylabone treats, hold off on those until you have finished brushing his entire body. This will give him something to look forward to at the end of each session.

Finish by combing through all the hair you have just brushed. As any groomer will tell you, the comb doesn't lie. If you can move a comb through your dog's entire coat easily, chances are good that you haven't missed any tangles.

CLIPPING AND STRIPPING

Owners of pet Springers usually trim their dogs' hair with clippers. Electric clippers, along with a variety of blades and other attachments, are sold at most pet supply stores. Although it is usually a bit more expensive, I strongly suggest going with a cordless model. The ease of being able to use your clippers virtually anywhere is well worth the added investment. I frequently do a quick touch-up on my own spaniels whenever I notice an imminent cowlick forming. This can also be a great way to lengthen the time between full grooming sessions.

The traditional English Springer Spaniel silhouette is instantly recognizable. To maintain this look, owners should clip the hair on the dog's face, neck, and back. The top third of each ear should also be trimmed. It may look easy, but clipping a dog is a true art form. Some owners show an instant talent, whereas others take months to fully master the task. Most clippers come with instructional videos filled with many useful tips for beginners.

Another very useful tool for a home groomer is a pair of thinning shears. A cross between a comb and a pair of scissors, thinning shears come in especially handy for blending the clipped area into a Springer's fringe. They are also very helpful for grooming dogs with particularly thick coats.

Most English Springer Spaniels competing in conformation are hand stripped. This means that the dead hair is pulled out with a stripping knife instead of being cut away. A show dog's head and neck are still usually trimmed with clippers, though. When done properly, hand stripping does not hurt a Springer, but some owners avoid stripping the hair from more delicate areas, such as bellies, using clippers there, as well.

Some owners who don't show their Springers still prefer to hand strip their dogs. Many simply prefer the more natural look that stripping provides. If you are considering hand stripping, however, be forewarned that it can be extremely time-consuming. Also, be sure to always strip your dog before bathing him, since it is harder to strip freshly

Getting Your Springer Used to Electric Clippers

Like other grooming tasks, clipping should begin as soon as you bring your English Springer Spaniel home. Of course, your Springer pup won't need a haircut each day, or even each week, but exposing him to this tool as often as possible is the best way to make him feel comfortable once it is time to use it. Let him sniff the clippers while they are off. To help your dog acclimate to the buzzing sound, turn the clippers on before ever touching him with them, being careful not to allow his nose near the blade.

The White Towel Test

If you use a white towel to dry your English Springer Spaniel after his bath, check it over for fleas and flea dirt before tossing it into your hamper. Both will appear as tiny dark specks. If you don't see any, your dog is probably flea-free. If you do see dark specks on the towel, contact your veterinarian.

washed hair. Grooming chalk can also help you get a better grip on your Springer's hair.

BATHING

Giving an English Springer Spaniel a bath is a lot like bathing a small child. You must gather all your materials before you begin, you should never leave your dog unattended in the tub, and you should expect to get at least a little wet yourself. Most Springers need a bath about once every four to six weeks. Owners of show dogs usually bathe their pets more frequently, as often as once a week.

Bathing Supplies

To bathe your Springer, you will need a quality canine shampoo and conditioner. Avoid using your own shampoo or bar soap on your pet. The pH levels of a dog's skin and hair are drastically different from our own; products made for humans will severely dry your Springer's coat. Numerous canine products are available at most pet supply stores.

Like shampoos for people, canine cleansers have become remarkably specialized in recent years. You can find shampoos and conditioners that contain natural ingredients like aloe vera and wheat germ oil to soothe and moisturize a dog's skin. They also come in a number of varieties and refreshing scents. There are also grooming sprays, ear washes, head-to-tail wipes, and other innovative multi-use items no owner should be without. I have used baby wipes on my pets for years, but the ones formulated specifically for dogs are even better.

In addition to shampoo and conditioner, you will also need ear cleanser and a handful of cotton balls. Expect to use several large and absorbent towels and at least one washcloth for each bath. If your shower doesn't have a spray nozzle, you will also need a cup for rinsing. It is much easier to rinse the coat thoroughly with a sprayer, though, so consider investing in one if you don't have one. Also, use a nonskid mat to keep your dog from slipping.

How to Bathe Your Springer Spaniel

Before running your dog's bath water, check the thermostat. Your dog will feel a bit chilly when he exits the tub, even in spring or fall. In summertime, set your air conditioning to a higher temperature than normal.

Place a cotton ball in each of your dog's ears, and then wet him down with tepid water. Some owners like filling the tub with water for their dogs' baths, but I prefer simply saturating my dogs' fur with the spray nozzle instead. The two minutes it takes the bath water to drain might not seem like a lot to you, but to your dog it can seem like an eternity.

Before you reach for your dog's shampoo, grab your washcloth and gently wipe his face with water alone. This reduces the chance of getting soap in his eyes. When you are finished, add some shampoo to the washcloth and work up a small lather before you begin cleaning his body. Canine shampoo doesn't create as many soap bubbles as human products, but applying the shampoo in this way will help distribute the cleanser evenly and also make rinsing easier.

Dry your Springer as best you can after his bath. An excessively damp coat will lead to painful knots.

Wash all areas: your dog's neck, chest, belly, back, legs, feet, and bottom.

Once you have shampooed your dog completely, you must rinse him thoroughly. This is the most important step in the bathing process, since leaving even small amounts of shampoo behind can lead to dry, itchy skin. A great way to be sure the job is done right is to rinse your Springer twice.

Next, squeeze a small amount of conditioner into your palm and rub it through your dog's coat. For specific information on the

amount and time to leave the product on, refer to the label. Some conditioners may be rinsed out almost immediately, while others should be left on for a few minutes to properly condition your Springer's hair and skin. Leave-in conditioners needn't be rinsed out at all.

Once you are done cleaning and conditioning your dog's skin (but before he leaves the tub), remove the cotton balls from his ears. This is an ideal opportunity to squirt a bit of cleanser into each ear and use a fresh cotton ball to remove dirt and excess wax. Just be sure this isn't the only time you perform this important task. (More on ear care in a moment.)

After his bath, towel-dry your dog to get as much water out of his fur as you can before blow drying. To prevent damaging the hair, squeeze the fur instead of rubbing it. A chamois cloth works especially well for this.

Some owners opt to let their Springers air-dry after baths, but if you choose to skip the dryer, be sure to brush your dog intermittently throughout the drying process. Wet fur has an uncanny ability to become tangled. Using a hair dryer also helps keep the coat from curling. Always use the lowest heat setting

There are many different nail trimmers available, and all are designed to cut your dog's nails easily.

when blow drying your Springer. Also, keep the appliance at least 12 inches (30 cm) from your dog to avoid skin burns. And be forewarned that your Springer's entire body will likely dry long before his ears.

NAIL TRIMMING

Even after years of practice, nail trimming is still my least favorite grooming task. I admit with no shame that I will defer nail trims to my husband or my dogs' veterinarian whenever I can. It's no wonder so many owners like me dread clipping their dogs' nails; no other chore is so ripe with potential for pain and bleeding. And at the risk of jinxing myself, I will add that I have never once injured one of my dogs when performing the task.

However, just because we don't enjoy nail trims, we mustn't postpone the task until our anxiety has passed. Your Springer Spaniel's nails must be trimmed at least once every two to three weeks regardless of how uncomfortable we may feel wielding those clippers. If you hear your dog's nails when he walks across the floor, he is already overdue for a trim.

Walking on overgrown nails can be extremely painful for your pet. Nails that are allowed to grow too long can also snag on carpet and clothing. This can cause the nail to be pulled completely out of the foot. This too can be incredibly painful and can also lead to infection.

Nail Trimming Supplies

At one time the tool used for nail trimming was mostly a matter of personal choice. Pliers-style, guillotine-style, and scissor-style clippers all work equally well, but many owners have a preference of one type over another. Today, however, the options go way beyond these traditional options.

If you want to avoid cutting the quick—that sensitive area deep in the nail, also called the nail bed—consider not cutting your Springer's nails at all. No, I'm not suggesting you skip the task; I'm referring to using a rotary grinding tool instead of conventional clippers. By grinding the nail down with this easy-to-use appliance, you are far less likely to remove too much of the nail. Grinders also leave smooth edges after each trim. If, by chance, you do make it down to the quick, the

Filing the Nails

If you use clippers, either traditional or electronic, use an emery board following your dog's trims to smooth the nail edges. If he won't tolerate this, taking him for brisk walks on asphalt or cement will have a similar effect. As one English Springer Spaniel breeder told me, one of the best ways to lengthen the time between nail trims is making sure your dog gets enough exercise.

wound will be instantly cauterized by the heat of the tool.

Another very smart tool is a new clipper that is electronically designed to sense the location of the nail bed. This amazing device can literally sense the blood vessels within the nail and alert you when you get too close to them with the clipper. Both this item and most rotary tools are battery-powered, making them easy to use virtually anywhere.

How to Trim Your Springer Spaniel's Nails

No matter what kind of nail trimmer you prefer, introduce it early. Show your puppy the device and let him sniff it over at least a few days before you need to trim his nails. This will make it a fairly familiar item when the time comes. Also, handle your Springer puppy's paws as often as possible. In many cases, a dog will pull away from having his nails trimmed not because of the trimmer itself, but because he doesn't like having his paws held. By touching his paws several times each day, you help avoid this problem.

If you are uncertain how to trim your dog's nails, ask your veterinarian to show you how.

When you are ready to trim your pet's nails, hold his foot firmly and press gently on the paw pad. This will extend the nails, so you can see them properly. Nail color can vary from dog to dog; one dog can have nails of different colors. If your Springer has lighter-colored nails, you may be able to see the quick. Black nails typically mask the nail bed, but this doesn't mean you will injure your pet. Simply proceed with caution.

Trim just the tip of the nail. If you decide the nail is too long, you can always go back and remove more, but you will never be able to reattach what you have trimmed away. Interestingly, removing just a small amount of the nail more frequently will encourage the nail bed to recede over time, making future trims much easier and considerably less stressful for all involved.

The Reluctant Subject

If your Springer resists nail trimming, be understanding but also adamant. If necessary, enlist the help of a family member to help hold your pet while you do the trimming. If he is a wriggler, this can help you avoid cutting him accidentally. Don't let your dog control the situation, though. You may only get a paw or two done this time around, but insist on trimming all the nails on at least one foot. Speak to your dog soothingly throughout the process, and try to end on a positive note. Also, consider offering him a small treat for each nail that you trim, at least while introducing the task. This will show him that nail trimming comes with rewards. Once he tolerates his nail trims better, you can reward him once for each foot you complete or once for the entire trim.

If You Keep Catching the Quick

If you find yourself repeatedly cutting the quick, pass the trimmers to someone else. Dogs can be amazingly forgiving creatures, but no animal should have to endure repeated injuries of any kind. Many veterinarians and professional groomers offer nail trimming services, usually for a nominal fee. My own vet doesn't even charge me for trimming nails when I bring my dogs for a routine visit.

EAR CARE

Like other breeds with pendant ears, English Springer Spaniels are prone to ear infections. Because their ear leather

Ear Hair

One way to increase air flow and reduce your dog's chance of infection is to keep the hair inside the ear trimmed. Clippers work wonderfully for this purpose. Some owners mistakenly believe that hair must be pulled from the ear. Never do this. Pulling the hair out can cause bleeding and infection. It is also extremely painful for your pet.

covers the opening to the ear canal, air flow to this area is severely restricted. This helps trap moisture, making the ear a natural breeding ground for bacteria. To help prevent infections, owners must clean their Springers' ears weekly.

Cleaning ears regularly also keeps your dog smelling good. A clean and healthy ear canal is whitish-pink, never brown or black. Dirty or infected ears may also emit a strong yeast or cheesy odor. If you suspect that your dog has an ear infection, skip the cleaning and go straight to the phone. He must see his veterinarian for diagnosis and treatment with antibiotics. If an infection is present, cleaning the ear will be painful for your pet. Since your vet will likely wish to swab the inside of the ear, introducing a cleaning solution could also make it more difficult for her to correctly identify the problem. Although it can be treated easily, an ear infection is a serious matter. Left untreated, it can even lead to hearing loss.

Because of the Springer's pendant ears, you must stay on top of cleaning them regularly. If not, your pet can get repeated ear infections.

Ear Cleaning Supplies

All you need to clean your English Springer Spaniels' ears is a bottle of ear cleaning solution and a handful of cotton balls. You can purchase ear cleanser at your local pet supply store, or you can mix a homemade solution from equal parts of vinegar and water. Always use cotton balls, never cotton swabs. Swabs can injure your Springer.

How to Clean Your English Springer Spaniel's Ears

Some dog owners clean their pets' ears by applying cleaning solution to a cotton ball and then wiping the ear. This falls short of getting the ear completely clean. To loosen and remove all dirt and excess wax, you must squirt the cleanser directly into the ear and then rub the outside gently. Most dogs resist the first step but bask in the second. If your dog shakes his head, don't worry. This will only help loosen the dirt and wax.

Next, using a clean cotton ball, wipe the inside of your dog's ear. Unlike a person's, the canine ear canal is L-shaped. This makes it unlikely that you will injure your dog by pushing the cotton in too far, but it is always important to be gentle nonetheless. Repeat the wiping process using fresh pieces of cotton each time. When the cotton comes out mostly clean, you know you are done. It needn't look pristine, though. A little wax left in the ear is not only acceptable, but it is also healthy.

Some owners do quick cleanings midweek with pre-moistened ear wipes. This is a great way to keep your Springer's ears clean and sweet smelling, but never assume that it replaces a thorough cleaning. Instead, think of wipes as providing helpful touch-ups between cleanings.

EYE CARE

Keeping your English Springer Spaniel's eyes clean and healthy is probably the simplest of all grooming tasks. All it takes is a few minutes each day. Simply wipe your dog's eyes with a soft, damp cloth to remove any debris that has settled into the eye area. If left to accumulate, eye discharge can harden and become difficult to remove from the hair on your dog's face.

Wiping your dog's eyes daily also offers you a regular opportunity to check his peepers for any problems. Always be

Eye Discharge

Springers are especially prone to eye discharge, so don't panic if there always seems to be some there to wipe from your dog's eyes. As you get used to performing this task, you will learn what and how much is normal for your pet. To keep discharge to a minimum, squirt a small amount of saline solution into each of your dog's eyes periodically.

on the lookout for redness, opaque or mucous-like discharge, or any apparent itching or squinting. If you notice any of these symptoms, consult your veterinarian. Simple problems like conjunctivitis (pink eye) can be cleared up quickly with medication. Unfortunately, problems with eyes can also signal more serious issues, such as progressive retinal atrophy (PRA) or neurological problems. Any changes in the pupil size or reactivity are a particular cause for concern. This makes it especially important to seek veterinary care as soon as you discover anything out of the ordinary.

DENTAL CARE

Good dental care begins with what you feed your English Springer Spaniel. Softer foods calcify, or turn into tartar, considerably faster than does harder fare. This doesn't mean you can't feed your dog wet food, but if you go this route, daily brushing is an absolute must. Ideally, even kibble eaters should have their pearly whites brushed as close to every day as possible. Big raw bones (never cooked, and never small bones) can also help remove plaque and tartar from your Springer's teeth, but you mustn't rely on these alone to get the job done. For a healthy mouth, brushing is a nonnegotiable task.

Toothbrushing Supplies

Canine toothbrushing supplies are available at most pet supply stores. Conventional

A Breath of Fresh Air

Before a case of doggy bad breath can be fixed, an owner must determine the cause. Most often plaque and tartar are to blame, but if your dog's teeth are clean and in good shape, the problem may be around his mouth, not inside it. Keeping your dog's flews (the pendulous upper folds of his lip) clean can help keep unpleasant odors to a minimum. Clipping this area often helps, as the hair at the very corner of the mouth can be a breeding ground for bacteria.

Offering your dog chew toys with breath freshening properties can also keep unpleasant odors from coming between you and your beloved English Springer Spaniel. A great way to improve your dog's breath without his even knowing it is to add a liquid breath freshener to his water bowl. This unique product can be added to water without changing its taste at all, but you'll definitely notice the difference.

Grooming Time Flies When You're Having Fun

Grooming tasks don't have to feel like chores. When you groom your English Springer Spaniel yourself, you deepen the bond between you and your pet through special time spent together. Tell your Springer how much you love him as you brush his coat each day. Give him a back rub before and after nail trimmings. Top off toothbrushing with an evening walk around the neighborhood. Soon your dog will look forward to these important tasks—and you just might start seeing them as more fun, as well.

toothbrushes along with sheath-style brushes that slip over an owner's finger are available along with toothpaste in popular all-in-one kits. You may also use a soft toothbrush made for a human child on your Springer, or you may even skip the brush altogether. When wet and placed on your finger, a square of gauze can also serve as a wonderful toothbrush and can be easier to get inside your dog's mouth if he resists the task.

Canine toothpaste, however, cannot be replaced with a product made for people. Our own toothpaste is made from ingredients that can make dogs sick. Canine toothpaste is meant to be swallowed, and comes in dog-friendly flavors like beef, liver, and chicken. The aromas alone can convince even a wary dog that toothbrushing may be a worthwhile activity after all. And he doesn't even have to wait until the job is done to get the treat.

Another item that many breeders recommend is a tooth scaler. Similar to the scraping device used by your own dentist, this tool helps remove any tartar that has already accumulated on your dog's teeth. Owners must be gentle, though. A Springer may tolerate a little scraping here and there, but if your dog

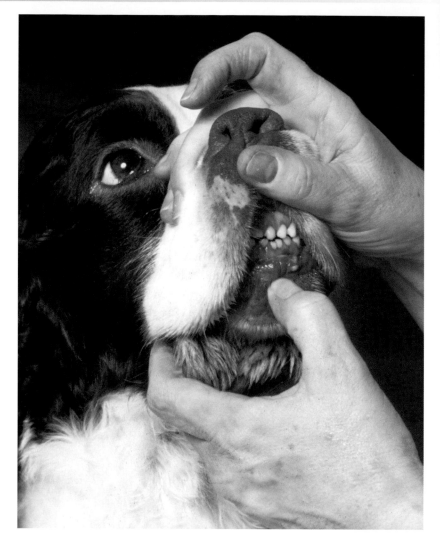

*Even your Springer needs
to have his teeth brushed!*

has a large amount of calculus, schedule a professional
cleaning instead.

The easiest way to avoid a professional tooth scaling
(which requires anesthesia) is by keeping up with your
Springer's dental care. This means brushing his teeth as often
as you can. Also, make sure your dog has ample opportunity
for chewing. Bones and other chew toys are a great (and fun)
way for your dog to keep his teeth looking and feeling good.

How to Brush Your English Springer Spaniel's Teeth

The best time to brush your English Springer Spaniels'
teeth is right after he has eaten his last meal of the day. Begin

by offering him a small amount of toothpaste on your finger. Once your Springer sees that the task involves this tasty treat, you shouldn't have a problem holding his attention. Getting him to embrace the toothbrush may still be a bit of a challenge, however. If your dog doesn't seem to mind the brush, squeeze a pea-size amount of toothpaste onto it. If you think the brush will interfere with his willingness to cooperate, grab the finger brush or gauze instead.

Beginning with your dog's top teeth, gently brush each tooth. Hold the brush at a 45-degree angle and move it in an oval or circular motion, paying special attention to the area where the tooth meets the gum. This is where plaque and tartar usually build up the most. Once you have finished the top teeth, repeat the procedure on your dog's bottom teeth. Although rinsing is not necessary with most canine toothpastes, I like to finish by offering my dogs a fresh drink of water.

Like most grooming tasks, toothbrushing works best when it is begun early and performed regularly. A dog who has never had his teeth brushed will be considerably more resistant than a Springer who regards it as just another part of the daily routine. If your dog is especially uncomfortable with the task, try setting smaller goals—perhaps working on his upper teeth one day and his lower teeth the next. The more you brush, the more comfortable he should become.

Good grooming habits set important precedents. By staying on top of all these important tasks, you help your dog accept them as jobs that simply must be done. You also show him that you care about his health and well-being. Your Springer might not understand the all the dirty details about ear infections or periodontal disease, but he will quickly learn that after being groomed, he always feels a little better.

6

TRAINING *and* BEHAVIOR
of Your English Springer Spaniel

ood behavior doesn't just happen: It is learned. Even when owners aren't aware of it, English Springer Spaniels are learning. Dogs constantly observe their environment and adjust their actions to better meet their needs. This is called latent learning. Sometimes latent learning leads a dog down the right path. After all, the world is full of natural consequences that are ripe with learning potential: When I corner the cat, she scratches me. At other times, though, what is learned isn't quite so helpful: When I beg, I get potato chips. By making training a part of your Springer puppy's routine, you help ensure that your dog is learning the things he should.

WHAT DOES MY SPRINGER NEED TO KNOW?

Not all English Springer Spaniels need formal training. Many household pets do just fine without ever knowing how to stay or heel on command. If you want to involve your Springer in an organized activity like conformation or obedience trials, however, a certain amount of formal training is a necessity. Even the most beautiful dogs are expected to behave properly in the show ring, and obedience trials require that each dog follow a detailed list of formal commands as proficiently as possible. If you have no interest in participating in activities like these with your dog, a certain amount of training is still sure to help you as a Springer owner.

Training teaches a dog discipline. More relaxed owners may cringe at this word. Many people confuse discipline with punishment. Please understand that discipline is not about reprimanding your dog for things he does wrong. It is about rewarding him for the things he does right so that he will repeat them. Are dogs capable of self-discipline? I would say yes, when they are properly trained. Your Springer may want to steal the filet that's sitting on your kitchen island waiting to head to the grill, but he will be much less likely to give in to the urge if he has been trained not to touch food that does not belong to him. My breeder can leave a TV tray in the middle of her living room with a plate of food on it when she leaves the room to answer the telephone, and not one of her dogs will touch it.

Active Learning

When your English Springer Spaniel is between six and ten months of age, expect a flurry of activity. This age for a Springer has been likened to a human child's terrible twos. Dogs are extremely energetic during this time period. American Kennel Club (AKC) judge and breeder Daniel Sena calls it the "age of terror." He added, "This is also the age where they learn the most and absorb the training vocabulary they'll retain for the rest of their lives."

You can use your Springer's innate desire to please you to your advantage with training.

Have a Clear Idea of What You Want to Train For

Before you can begin training your dog, you must define your objective. Perhaps your expectations lie somewhere between creating a couch potato and fashioning a Westminster champion. This is a very realistic goal, and teaching your new Springer puppy a few simple commands is a great starting point.

Many trainers offer beginner classes in which owners can come together to work with their puppies in a common location. An added benefit to this approach is that the dogs (and the people) reap some extra socialization time in the process. The goals of puppy kindergarten really aren't that different from kindergarten for kids. During this phase, the students learn about good manners and how to play nicely with each other.

If you started daydreaming about blue ribbons as soon as you saw the word "Westminster," you should keep these ambitious goals in mind when searching for a trainer. Look for someone with experience in training show dogs specifically. You will still want to start by enrolling your Springer puppy in a beginner's class, but your goals for this introductory training phase will be quite different from the average pet owner. Since there is no doubt that you will be moving on after puppy kindergarten, you may also want to find a trainer who offers classes at all levels of training. Few dogs make it all the way to a Westminster show, but if a Best in Show

Using Positive Reinforcement

For your pet, positive reinforcement may include food treats, praise, petting, or a favorite toy or game. Food treats work especially well in training your dog. A treat should be enticing and irresistible to your pet. It should be a very small, soft piece of food so that she will immediately gulp it down and look to you for more. If you give her something she has to chew or that breaks into bits and falls on the floor, she'll be looking at the floor, not at you. Small pieces of soft commercial treats, hot dogs, cheese, or cooked chicken or beef have all proven successful. Experiment a bit to see what works best for your pet. You can carry the treats in a pocket or fanny pack. Each time you use a food reward, couple it with a verbal reward (praise). Say something like, "Good dog," in a positive, happy tone of voice.

Some pets may not be interested in food treats. For those pets, the reward could be in the form of a toy or brief play.

When your pet is learning a new behavior, she should be rewarded every time she does the behavior, which means continuous reinforcement. It may be necessary to use a technique called shaping with your pet, which means reinforcing something close to the desired response and then gradually requiring more from your dog before she gets the treat. For example, if you're teaching your dog to shake hands, you may initially reward her for lifting her paw off the ground, then for lifting it higher, then for touching your hand, then for letting you hold her paw, and finally, for actually "shaking hands" with you.

Intermittent reinforcement can be used once your pet has reliably learned the behavior. At first, reward her with the treat three out of every four times she does the behavior. Then, over time, reward her about half the time, then about a third of the time, and so on, until you're only rewarding her occasionally with the treat. Continue to praise her every time—although once your dog has learned the behavior, your praise can be less effusive, such as a quiet, but positive, "Good dog." Use a variable schedule of reinforcement so that she doesn't catch on that she only has to respond every other time. Your pet will soon learn that if she keeps responding, eventually she'll get what she wants—your praise and an occasional treat.

(Courtesy of the Humane Society of the United States)

win is your dream, you should stack the odds in your dog's favor from the beginning.

How to Find a Trainer

Ask your Springer's breeder or veterinarian to recommend a reputable dog trainer in your area. You may also contact the Association of Pet Dog Trainers at (800) PET-DOGS or www.apdt.com for the name of a trainer near you. Avoid using the phone book or bulletin board advertisements. Dog trainers do not have to be licensed to perform the work they do, so owners must use extreme care in the selection process. If you do go with someone without a personal or professional

Anyone can claim to be a trainer. Ask for references, professional certifications, and recommendations.

recommendation, ask for references, and be sure to follow up by checking them.

The best dog trainers teach owners how to successfully train their pets themselves. In this way, a trainer is really more a teacher. Since you will be learning right along with your Springer, it is vital that both you and your dog are comfortable with the person you choose. A trainer should always be willing to answer any questions you may have and explain things without talking down to you.

It is important to note that different trainers utilize different forms of training. Popular methods include leash and collar, reward-based, and clicker training techniques. Any of these methods can help your Springer grow into a happy and well-behaved canine companion. Whatever form of training you choose, make sure the trainer never uses physical punishment of any kind. Training should always be a positive activity for your dog.

TRAINING WITH THE WHOLE FAMILY

Training your English Springer Spaniel is not only an important job, but it also can be a fun activity for your entire family. Involving each family member in the training process is good for your pet, too. Just as a dog should learn to respond to you and not just a professional trainer, your Springer should also work with different people to ensure his compliance even when the person he considers his master isn't present.

I learned this the hard way. My first Spaniel, Jonathan, would only follow commands from me—because I was the only person who ever trained him. When I met my husband Scot, I discovered that I had created a bit of a monster. When Scot would instruct Jonathan to do something, Johnny would immediately turn to me, as if asking whether he had to comply or not. As soon as I repeated the command, however, he would comply. Ultimately, I solved this problem by leaving Jonathan in Scot's care regularly so that they could do some remedial training together. We were lucky in that this didn't take too long or present any major challenges, but this isn't always the case for dogs with this type of training tunnel vision for their owners. Exposing your Springer to as many masters as possible during his initial training period is a highly preferable option.

Kids can also be wonderful helpers in the training process. Even the youngest child can praise a dog or reward him for performing a task with a treat. Just be sure your kids are dispensing both at the appropriate moment. A smart strategy is to begin teaching your Springer a particular task or command yourself. Once your dog catches on, your son or daughter may

Man's (and Woman's) Best Friend

Well-socialized dogs are welcomed in far more places than dogs who show fear and aggression around people. If you expose your English Springer Spaniel to as many people and animals as possible throughout his puppyhood, he will be much more likely to grow into a social adult. Socializing must be done both early and regularly, though, for the task to be successful and for the benefits to be lasting.

Socializing a Springer puppy is one of the easiest parts of training. Simply bring your dog with you wherever you go, whenever you can. Take him to parks, playgrounds, sporting events—virtually anywhere that allows dogs and where lots of people gather. Invite strangers to meet your dog, and be sure to bring along some tasty treats for these new friends to offer him. This will help him view meeting new people as a rewarding activity.

If a particular person isn't wild about interacting with your Springer, move on to someone who shows more interest. Although I can't understand it myself, certain people simply do not like dogs. Some even fear them. It is extremely important that we respect everyone's feelings. Spending time trying to coax a nondog lover into patting your Springer will do little more than annoy the person—and it will likely raise a red flag with your dog. Dogs are extremely intuitive individuals. You want your Springer's experiences with people to be as positive as possible.

Invite friends and family members to your home regularly. Make a point of exposing your dog to both adults and children, but for safety's sake always supervise any interactions involving kids. Your Springer may be the gentlest animal you've ever known, but not all children are good with pets. A negative experience with a child could leave your Springer with the mistaken impression that all kids are bad news.

If a friend invites you to his home, ask if you may bring your Springer. If you work in a dog-friendly setting, ask your boss if you may bring your dog to work with you once in a while. My friend brings her dog with her to her local library, where they are always met with cheerful greetings and dog biscuits from the library staff. Of course, not all public places are so accommodating, but it never hurts to ask if you can bring your dog in with you. Remember, the more socialized your Springer is, the more likely the people are to say yes.

If every member of your family spends equal time training your Springer, he will listen to everyone and not just to the commands given by one person.

then practice the exercise to reinforce the command.

CRATE TRAINING

If you wish to crate train your English Springer Spaniel, it is extremely important that you start the process as soon as you bring your new puppy home. This means you must have your dog's crate ready for him on homecoming day. If you wait even a few weeks to let him adjust to his new environment, he will acclimate to the new setting without the crate being part of it. If you use the crate from the very first day, your Springer will accept the crate as part of the woodwork, so to speak. Trying to introduce this item at a later time will only make it more difficult for him—and for you.

Few dog training subjects elicit such strong reactions from owners as crate training. Some owners swear by this training

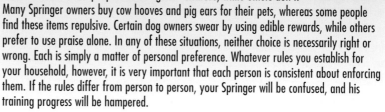

Get on the Same Page

If several family members will be participating in training your Springer, be sure everyone understands the ground rules clearly. Each household is a bit different. Some people allow dogs on furniture, while others don't. Many Springer owners buy cow hooves and pig ears for their pets, whereas some people find these items repulsive. Certain dog owners swear by using edible rewards, while others prefer to use praise alone. In any of these situations, neither choice is necessarily right or wrong. Each is simply a matter of personal preference. Whatever rules you establish for your household, however, it is very important that each person is consistent about enforcing them. If the rules differ from person to person, your Springer will be confused, and his training progress will be hampered.

method, while others see it as cruel. The good news is that crating is an option. If you don't wish to crate your Springer, there is no reason you must. But if you want to give your dog a quiet place of his own, and reap the housetraining rewards that accompany this training method, crate training just may be for you.

Is Crate Training Right for You?

Before you begin crate training your English Springer Spaniel, you must decide if your dog is indeed a good candidate for crating. For example, my Spaniel Molly came from a breeder a couple towns away from where I live. I met her when she was just four weeks old, and she had been exposed to crates at the breeder's home. All the breeder's dogs had one, and although Molly hadn't been kept in one herself, she saw the adult dogs go to them whenever it was time to eat or sleep. To her, this wasn't an unusual or negative item at all. I eventually bought Molly a crate of her own to stop her from sleeping under the desk in my office on of all the computer cables, and she adapted to it easily and happily.

Crates as Caves

Crate enthusiasts often compare the crate to the den-like environments wild dogs seek out in the nature. Molly's fondness for the cramped space under my work desk could reasonably stem from this natural canine instinct. As Ted Kerasote explained in his book *Merle's Door*, however, such claims must be put in perspective. In wild wolf packs, for instance, the alpha female is the only wolf to regularly occupy the den. And even she only settles there long enough to give birth and nurse the pups. A crate is not something that every dog needs—or wants.

Crating Concerns

If Molly had been purchased from a pet store or adopted through rescue, I would have given my decision to crate her a bit more thought. Many dogs who began their lives in puppy mills do not accept crates as easily as Molly did. Because they spent most of their time in these small enclosures, many puppy mill dogs are extremely uneasy with being crated. Also, little potential exists for crating to help with housetraining these dogs, since they have already been forced to overcome their innate distaste for soiling the area in which they sleep.

Likewise, if your rescued Springer was mistreated by being kept for too long in a crate, steering clear of crating is probably the best decision. Even a well-adjusted dog may fuss or whine in the crate during the early stages of crate training, but a dog with a history of abuse involving the crate presents an entirely different situation. Crating should provide a stress-free refuge for dogs; it should never induce panic or a similarly intense reaction.

Occasionally, even a dog who hasn't had a negative experience with a crate may have an adverse reaction to being crated. If this happens to your Springer, I recommend skipping the crating process. Like people, dogs are individuals. One of our most important duties as owners is watching our dogs' reactions and respecting their feelings when a choice causes them distress.

How To Crate Train Your English Springer Spaniel

Begin crate training by doing nothing more than allowing your dog to investigate this item. Assemble the crate before bringing your new Springer home, and place a toy inside it. When he enters the crate, reward him with a treat. This will help

While your Springer is still a puppy, be prepared to take him outside regularly to eliminate.

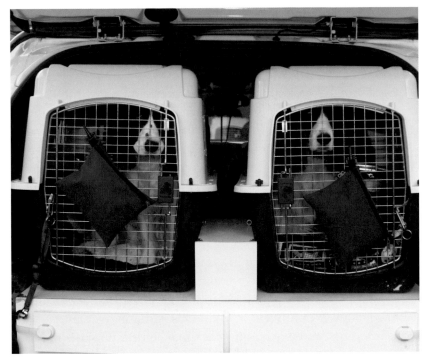

Crate training your Springer may get him to easily adapt to car travel.

him form a positive connotation to the enclosure. Hold off on closing the door, though. For the first few days, simply leave the door open and keep the treats coming. Whenever you give your dog a treat, in fact, do so in the crate. Don't be surprised if your Springer starts running to his crate when he hears his cookie jar rattle. (Both of mine do.)

Once your dog is entering his crate regularly, begin closing the door for short periods of time. This is when you are most likely to encounter some resistance. If your dog cries or barks, wait to open the door until he stops. He must not make a connection between whimpering and being released. In the beginning, you will only be closing the door for a minute or two at the most, so it shouldn't be hard to wait for a break in any vocalization or pawing at the door before letting him out. Ending on a good note is imperative to your success. Also, remember to praise him lavishly. Repeat this exercise several times each day, gradually increasing the time your dog stays inside the crate.

Once your Springer is tolerating being left inside the crate for five minutes or more, you may then begin leaving the room immediately after placing him in the crate. Again, gradually

increase the amount of time he is left inside. This is also a common point of resistance. If your dog howls when you leave the room, do not return until he has stopped. Wait for the break, or you will reward the wrong behavior.

Continue to leave your dog's crate open so that he may enter it at any time he wishes. Like treats, new toys should also be given to your pet inside the crate. Eventually, you may find your dog resting or even gnawing on a chew toy inside his kennel. This is proof positive that he has accepted the crate as his own personal sanctuary.

HOUSETRAINING

Of all the training tasks you will perform with your English Springer Spaniel, housetraining him is likely the one you look forward to the least. You're not alone. Few owners enjoy cleaning up after accidents or standing out in the cold waiting for their dogs to finally get it. While it's certainly true that housetraining can be frustrating at times, it doesn't have to be difficult.

Make a Schedule

You can speed up housetraining with one simple resource: a schedule. Sticking to a routine will decrease the amount of time you spend on housetraining considerably. This means feeding your Springer at the same times each day and taking him to his potty spot every two hours until he is eight weeks old. No matter how smart or trainable your dog is, at this age, his bladder simply cannot go any longer between eliminating. For every additional month of age, a puppy should be able to wait another hour between elimination trips. So, a three-month-old puppy can go three hours between trips, and a four-month-old can wait four hours. This reaches a reasonable limit once your dog is about six to eight months old. No dog should ever wait more than eight hours without being given a chance to relieve himself.

Utilize the Crate

If you are using a crate with your Springer, place him inside it whenever you cannot watch him while housetraining him. This will help prevent accidents. Be sure to fetch him and take him to his potty spot when the scheduled time approaches, though, or the biological need to eliminate will kick in. When your Springer is outside his crate, constantly be on the lookout for signs that he needs to eliminate. Most dogs have pre-elimination habits, such as circling an area or sniffing for the right spot. If you see your puppy do either of these things, take him to his proper potty spot immediately.

Cleaning Up Accidents

If you find an accident on the floor of your home (and you will—at least a few times), remove your dog from the room while you clean it up. Watching you remove the waste and cleanse the area may give your dog the impression that his job is to make the messes and yours is to clean them up. Again, the crate can serve as a useful item in this instance. If you aren't use a crate, simply place him in another (puppy-proofed) room and close the door or use a safety gate to keep him from observing the clean-up phase.

Be sure to clean the area of the accident thoroughly. Your dog will be much more likely to repeat the offense if he smells any remnants from his first accident. For wet messes, absorb the urine with a rag or paper towel until there is absolutely no liquid left. Then wash the area with an odor-eliminating cleaner. These are sold at most pet supply stores, and most work quite

Never punish a dog for housetraining accidents. It won't help the process and can damage your relationship with your Springer.

Make a Chart

When I am housetraining a puppy, I post a housetraining chart on my refrigerator. On it, I keep track of the dog's meals, successful trips to the potty spot, and accidents. If your household is as busy as mine, it can be easy to forget exactly what time you fed your Springer or when he last went outside. A chart can also bolster your confidence in your pet as you literally see the proof that he is having fewer and fewer housetraining mishaps. If you find that your Springer loves to go outside and walk — but he doesn't seem to understand that trips outside are also for elimination, try using a different leash for walks than for housetraining trips. This can help your dog differentiate between a trip outdoors for a leisurely stroll and one to do his business.

well. Avoid cleaners containing ammonia. Since urine naturally contains this compound, your dog may smell the ammonia and mistake the area cleaned with it for an acceptable potty spot.

To help your Springer understand where you want him to eliminate, transport a small amount of solid waste from his most recent accident to his potty spot. You may also place the urine-soaked towel you used when cleaning up for this same purpose. At the end of the day, clean your dog's potty spot, removing these items. Both urine and feces contain bacteria that can potentially spread disease if left to accumulate.

When Dogs Need to Go

In the beginning, you may feel like all you are doing is taking your dog outside—often to no avail. Hang in there! As your Springer gets just a little older and starts to catch on to eliminating in the right spot, your trips outdoors will become more successful and less frequent. Most dogs need to empty their bladders and bowels first thing in the morning, before going to bed at night, shortly after eating meals, and upon waking from naps. A dog should also be given an opportunity to relieve himself before being crated and immediately after being released from the crate. This may still seem like many trips, but most owners fall into an easy routine within the first few months of housetraining success.

Teaching Your Dog to Tell You When He Needs to Go

You may teach your Springer to let you know when he needs to go to his potty spot by placing a bell or other noise-making device near the door. I use a yellow cow bell for my Spaniels. Each time you take your dog to his potty spot, gently lift his

Weigh Your Words

English Springer Spaniels can be very sensitive animals. This makes it extremely important for owners to train their dogs using only positive reinforcement. Even a verbal admonishment can have a negative effect. As one breeder told me, "One harsh word can destroy months of training and trust."

paw to ring the bell before heading outdoors. Soon he will learn that ringing the bell means getting to go outside to eliminate.

Remember to Praise Your Dog

The best way to encourage your Springer to eliminate in the proper area is praising him when he succeeds. Punishing him in any way will only deter your dog's progress. More importantly, never strike your dog or rub his nose in excrement to teach him that eliminating in the house is wrong. All you will teach you beloved pet by doing either of these things is to fear you.

LEASH TRAINING

All English Springer Spaniels should know how to walk on a leash properly. This means walking alongside their owners at a similar pace. If a puppy is allowed to pull in any direction, he will soon learn that pulling enables him to go wherever he chooses. Walking a Springer puppy who pulls may not seem like a big problem, but along with your dog, the problem will only get bigger. It will be much harder to win the tug of war with an adult dog.

Taking your Springer for a walk every day is a simple and easy way for the two of you to get some exercise and to bond.

If you have rescued a Springer who was never taught how to walk on leash, I suggest using a head harness instead of a conventional collar with your dog's leash. This clever item has been described as being like power steering for dogs. It enables an owner to control the direction the dog faces. This can come in extremely handy if your dog is easily distracted by scampering squirrels or leaves blowing around in the wind. A head harness also pulls the dog's head down if he pulls, effectively discouraging the behavior.

Perhaps you have a large, fenced backyard and see no reason for even using a leash on your Springer. Inevitably, though, situations will arise in which your dog needs to be leashed. When your

One Step Forward

If you live in a single-level home or in a building with an elevator, consider taking your English Springer Spaniel puppy to a stadium or other public place with steps to teach him how to climb and descend stairways. He may not need to walk up and down stairs at home, but if he is never presented with the opportunity as a pup, he may balk at the idea as an adult.

Begin by walking up just one or two stairs with your dog. Praise him and offer him a treat for complying, and then direct him to walk back down. Repeat this exercise using just one or two steps until your dog seems comfortable walking both up and down stairs. You may then increase the number of steps you tackle together gradually. Once he has mastered the task, consider taking the stairs the next time you go to push that elevator button. Step climbing is great exercise for both you and your Springer.

dog visits his veterinarian, for example, a leash protects him from vehicles outside and from other animals inside the hospital. Also, even a dog with the most luxurious backyard deserves a change of scenery once in a while. Chasing a ball at home may provide your dog with sufficient exercise, but it doesn't afford the same pleasure as touring the neighborhood and visiting with friends along the way. A leash gives a dog the opportunity to be social, and most Springers are very social creatures indeed.

A dog who hasn't been walked on a leash regularly may fear having a lead attached to his collar. To prevent this from happening, make walks a part of your Springer's daily routine from the very beginning. You don't have to go far; short walks can be just as fun and efficient for leash training as long ones. If your dog reacts to the leash with anxiety, place it on the floor in front of him so that he can inspect it freely. Next, hook it to his collar and let him walk around indoors with the lead attached. As you move on to venturing outside with your dog on the leash, he will likely start to see it for exactly what it is—a simple item that can yield loads of enjoyment.

BASIC OBEDIENCE

Obedience. Even the word sounds somewhat intimidating, doesn't it? For owners with little or no experience, formal obedience training may even seem a bit like canine boot camp. I have no desire to control my dogs' every move by constantly telling them when to sit or when to speak. One of the things I like best about my own dogs is the fact that they are individuals. I actually like how my male Spaniel, Damon, sometimes talks back when I give him a command. He always complies, but he frequently mumbles under his breath to let me know he doesn't really want to do what I have instructed. Molly, on the other hand, delights in following obedience commands. As stubborn as she is, she loves learning new things and showing off how much she knows. Thankfully, this is what obedience training is truly about: learning how to properly communicate with your dog. Although some owners do try to make it about control, obedience training works best when both dog and owner are working together toward a common goal.

The biggest advantage to obedience training your English

Springer Spaniel is that it can protect your dog from harm. If you teach your Springer just one command, train him to come to you when called. Complying could literally save his life one day if he ever escapes the safety of your home or yard. Unless you plan to enter your dog in obedience trials, you do not have to teach him every command in the training play book, but each one does come with its own benefit.

Teaching your Springer the *drop-it* command can prevent him from eating disgusting items he encounters while walking outdoors. The *leave-it* command can make it so that he never touches these items in the first place. To my dismay, my own dogs seem to have radar for finding wads of used chewing gum and other filthy items in public places, so I have found both these commands undeniably helpful.

Obedience also helps teach good manners. If you teach your Springer to sit before you open the door of your home to guests, your dog will be much less likely to jump on your visitors. Teaching your dog to heel can prevent him from delivering an overly excited greeting to friends and neighbors you encounter

Owners (and Safety) First

Always walk through a door before allowing your English Springer Spaniel to walk through it. In addition to teaching your dog good manners, this also keeps both of you safe. An overly zealous Springer can unintentionally cause an owner to fall. He can also escape if he ever finds himself in front of an open door. If your dog tries to race his way over the threshold, pull him back and command him to sit and stay. Practice this exercise as many times as it takes for your Springer to wait for his turn to exit the door.

Training your dog will allow you to control his behavior and prevent him from getting into anything you don't want him in or near.

while walking him. Obedience training can even discourage a dog from reacting aggressively in a number of situations.

Obedience training may be done in a group setting or privately in your own backyard. Likewise, you may utilize the help of a professional dog trainer (many make house calls) or oversee the task yourself. Books and instructional videos on canine obedience training can be found at most pet supply stores and book stores.

While teaching the following commands, always reward your Springer for his compliance. Even if he only accomplishes part of the task, praise him for every move in the right direction. You may also choose to use edible rewards to reinforce what your dog learns. Food can serve as a powerful motivator when it comes to training. Nothing, however, can replace heartfelt praise.

The Hunting Springer

If you plan to hunt with your Springer, obedience training is a must. Since your dog needs to be off-leash to do this kind of work, it is vital that he consistently comply with any commands you give him. In this situation, a formal class for field dogs may be the best plan.

Once your dog is consistently complying with a specific command—at least 85 percent of the time—start offering the edible rewards only intermittently. You do not want your dog to perform the task only when a treat is offered. Dispense verbal praise as often as you like, though. I always praise my own dogs for complying with commands. Perhaps this is why Damon obeys me even when he would rather do something else.

Conversely, never punish your dog for taking too long to learn a particular command. Punishing him will only deter him from further learning. If you remain both patient and consistent, your Springer will catch on eventually. Work on one command at a time until your dog masters each task. And be sure to limit training to reasonable time periods. Your Springer will learn the most by working with you for short time periods (ideally from 5 to 15 minutes) several times each day.

Also, remember that the information in this book is a guideline for training. You may change small parts of the strategies if doing so works better for either you or your dog. When teaching your Springer commands, though, avoid using any more syllables in the words than necessary. Unless you plan to enter your dog in obedience trials, there is no reason you must use the word "stay" for instance. But if you try to teach your dog to respond to the longer phrase—"Stay right there"—it will be harder for him to learn the desired behavior. Keeping things simple is always best. If you wish to replace this conventional command with another word, try using "wait" instead. My husband and I used this command when training our own dogs because they seemed to respond better to the hard consonant at the end of the word. Similarly, avoid using phrases such as "lie down" or "come here."

Come

The easiest way to teach your dog to come to you is by catching him in the act. Whenever you notice him moving toward you, say the word "come" in a cheerful voice. It is very important that you praise your dog for complying with this command. Never scold your Springer when he comes to you—even if he has done something to make you unhappy. If your dog fears coming to you, he may not comply. In an emergency situation, this could be very dangerous.

Treats and pats, hugs, and love will make training a fun, rewarding experience for your Springer.

When you practice the *come* command more formally, I recommend using a leash or asking a friend to join you. It is extremely important that your Springer come to you when the command is issued. If you have no means of making him do so, what he will learn is that he does not have to comply with it. Retractable leashes come in quite handy in this situation, as do edible rewards. I have also found that kneeling and opening my arms helps encourage my own dogs to come to me. Some trainers say that this position mimics that of the canine play bow, the posture a dog uses to initiate play with other animals.

If you want your dog to always come to you when called, never chase him, not even in a playful way. You don't want your dog to ever mistake an emergency situation for a game of hide-and-seek in which he should hide from you. If you wish to play hide-and-seek with your Springer, always let your dog be the seeker. This too can be a practical way of reinforcing the *come* command. Once you have hidden, call out to your dog and ask him to come find you. And be sure to reward him for winning the game.

Sit

Sit is usually one of the easiest commands for a dog to learn. It is also the basis for many other commands, so be sure to teach this one early. Many breeders work on teaching their puppies to sit before they are even old enough to go home with their new families. If you want to see something cute, watch a breeder who has taught the *sit* command open a bag of puppy treats. Nothing makes those little bottoms hit the floor faster!

If your Springer doesn't know the *sit* command, begin by holding a treat over his head and moving it forward as you tell him to sit. Most dogs respond by naturally moving into the sit position. If yours does not, do not push on his back or bottom. This can put too much pressure on his legs and back. Instead, push gently on both his back legs, just behind the knee. This will compel him to sit without hurting him.

Down

Once your Springer knows how to sit, you may then teach him the *down* command. While he is still in the *sit* position, place a treat in your hand and slowly draw it down toward the floor as you say the word "down." As soon as your dog lowers his body to get the treat, offer it to him along with praise for complying.

You must make sure your dog doesn't rely on the physical

Punishing your dog for not following a command correctly may do more harm than good.

gesture of lowering your hand, though. Once he begins to grasp this command, gradually begin limiting how far down you move your hand as you issue the command. Eventually, you won't need to use the visual cue at all.

Stay

Stay is another command for which sitting is a prerequisite. With your dog sitting, raise your hand in a stop-sign gesture and say the word "stay." As soon as you say the word, begin moving backward just a bit. In the very beginning, your Springer may only stay still for a second or two, but this is still progress. Remember, be patient! Be sure to reward him while he is still in the process of staying, though, or you will be rewarding him for the wrong behavior.

As you work on this command more and more, your dog will stay still for longer and longer periods. As he does, gradually increase both the distance you move back and the time between issuing the command and providing the reward. Eventually, you should be able to expect your dog to stay put for about a minute with you about 10 feet (3 m) away.

Heel

If you plan to show your Springer, you must teach him the *heel* command. This command can also be extremely useful if you regularly take your dog for walks on his leash. The beauty of this command is that, once properly taught, you hardly ever have to say the actual word anymore. What heeling basically means is walking on a leash politely, never pulling, and sitting patiently whenever the person holding the leash stops.

You may be tempted to skip teaching this command, because it seems a bit complicated. I promise, though that it's not as hard as it may sound. To best teach this command, I recommend using a proven training method called task analysis. By breaking any multi-part task down into smaller, more manageable steps, a dog learns each one separately and can then use them together. This helps set your dog up for success.

Begin by teaching your Springer to sit. This command must be mastered before tackling heeling. Next, work on getting your Springer comfortable with his leash. An aversion to the leash can interfere greatly with teaching the *heel* command. Allow some time for your dog to acclimate to these two tasks before moving on to the next. Expecting a Springer puppy to learn how to sit, tolerate a leash, and heel all in the same week is simply too large a job for either the dog or his owner.

If your dog pulls while being walked, simply stand still. Most dogs will turn around to see why their owners have stopped; this effectively interrupts the pulling. Resume walking, continuing to stop whenever your Springer pulls you. If your dog keeps pulling repeatedly, change your direction to show him that it won't get him where he wants to go. Constant pulling can hurt your dog's throat and also can injure you, so it is extremely important that you correct this problem, even if you have no plans for teaching him the full *heel* command.

The drop-it *and* leave-it *commands are important to teach your Springer because they can very well save his life if he attempts to eat something he's not supposed to.*

The next to last step in teaching your dog to heel is issuing the sit command whenever you stop during a walk. Be sure to stop at different points in your route each time. Finally, with your dog's leash in your right hand and a treat in your left, say the word "heel" as soon as your Springer sits, and then

immediately offer the edible reward along with praise. Timing is crucial for this important last step.

At first you will need to issue the sit command before the *heel* command. After some practice, however, your dog will respond to the word "heel" alone. Eventually, he will freely stop and sit whenever you stop walking. Once your Springer has mastered heeling in his own neighborhood, venture out to different places for practice. Teaching your dog to follow commands in strange environments and amid new distractions is a true training accomplishment.

Drop It/Leave It

The best tool for teaching the *drop-it* and *leave-it* commands is your dog's favorite toy. He must be wild about the item in order for the training to be most effective. To get started, offer your Springer the toy and encourage him to play with it. Once he is immersed in the sound of the squeaker or the taste of mint on his dental chew, pick the item back up as you say the words "drop it." At first he may not want to relinquish the item. He may even hold onto it a bit tighter when you reach for it, but some gentle coaxing with an edible reward should change his mind. As soon as he drops the toy, offer the treat and praise him for letting go. Practice this exercise over and over until he readily drops the object. I also suggest using other favorite items so that your Springer learns that the command applies to any item he may currently possess. I once saved Molly from eating a human multivitamin that I accidentally dropped onto the floor when I issued the *drop-it* command. Her immediate response was to pick it up, but she readily let it fall back to the floor when I used this one phrase.

Teaching the *leave-it* command is very similar to training a dog to drop a particular item. Instead of giving the toy to your Springer, however, in this case you should set it on the floor near him. As soon as he moves toward the item, say the words "leave it" and offer him a treat for his compliance. As with the former command, repeating the exercise will be necessary. This command is useful for keeping your dog from touching something he shouldn't—like that runaway vitamin. Unfortunately, I wasn't quick enough to use the *leave-it* command, so this is an excellent example of why teaching both commands is a smart move.

PROBLEM BEHAVIORS

When a dog behaves badly, there is almost always a reason. If your Springer is chewing inappropriate items, for instance, he may be bored, or he might be reacting to some type of stress in his environment. If your dog barks or howls excessively when he is alone, he may be in need of some canine companionship. Some reasons for bad behavior are more obvious than others, but looking at the situation from all angles before reacting is a wise step.

First, check with your veterinarian to make sure your Springer's problem isn't health related. When a dog is in pain, he is much more likely to act out through inappropriate behavior. Your vet can help you create a strategy for dealing with a behavior problem once a physical cause has been ruled out.

Next, ask yourself if your dog is getting enough exercise. Pent-up energy can lead to a number of behavior problems. Lack of socialization also can lead to behavior issues. If you live

If your dog is acting aggressively toward people or other dogs, you must correct this behavior immediately.

Rage Syndrome

Several different types of canine aggression exist. A dog may act aggressively to show dominance, as a response to fear, from training as a guard dog, or as a means of protecting his own territory. Over the years, English Springer Spaniels displaying severe aggression problems have been said to be suffering from rage syndrome. This extreme form of aggression has been documented most frequently in English Springer Spaniels and English Cocker Spaniels, but it can occur in any breed. It is not called Springer rage, as some people mistakenly refer to it.

Extensive research has been done on the subject, including a groundbreaking study at Cornell University headed by Ilana Riesner, DVM. In the English Springer Spaniel breed, so-called rage syndrome was found to actually be a form of dominance aggression in most situations. It was also discovered that the most severe cases could be linked to a common bloodline. Dominance aggression is most common in show lines.

Most dogs give at least some warning before biting—a stare, growling, or a curled lip exposing the teeth, for example. In contrast, this more intense form of aggression is characterized by sudden, unprovoked attacks. When faced with a situation he finds threatening, the dog lacks vital impulse control. He reacts immediately, whether the perceived threat is legitimate or not.

Perhaps most importantly, Riesner's study identified a common physiological cause for the problem: abnormally low levels of serotonin in the brain. This same abnormality has been linked to violence in human mental health patients and prison inmates. Dogs suffering from severe aggression can be treated with medications that increase serotonin levels. Whether a dog will respond positively to treatment and ongoing training depends on several factors, including the age of the dog when the problem began and the severity of the aggression.

near a dog park with appropriate fencing, I strongly recommend taking your Springer for some fun, off-leash play time. Dogs need untethered playtime to build strong muscles, but this free exercise also keeps them mentally healthy. If there are no dog parks in your area, check into a doggy daycare program that offers physical activities. Enrolling your Springer for just a day or two each week could make a huge difference in how he acts at home. Although these two things may at first seem completely unrelated, running around with other dogs for just a couple of hours each week could eliminate your dog's barking problem when you must leave him home alone.

In extreme situations, your veterinarian may recommend treating your dog with an antidepressant medication to help with a behavior problem. Fluoxetine, a selective serotonin reuptake inhibitor (SSRI) that is also prescribed for people, has been shown to produce a calming effect in canine patients, making them more receptive to training. It is important to note, however, that canine and human patients have something significant in common when it comes to pharmacological treatment: Without environmental enrichment, the results of the medication will likely fall short of their potential. In other words, antidepressants will only help if dog owners are willing to offer their pets opportunities for exercise and socialization, as well.

Aggression

If your dog is displaying signs of aggression, a dog park or daycare is not the answer. Only dogs with reliable dispositions should be taken to dog parks. Likewise, daycare providers will gladly accept dogs with good temperaments in an effort to curb such behavioral issues as chewing or barking, but they must draw the line at aggression, since it puts their other canine clients and staff members at risk. In this case, seek the advice of a professional trainer or an animal behavior specialist, but still talk to your veterinarian first.

Puppies need to chew, so make sure you provide lots of chew toys for your Springer.

Aggression should always be treated as a serious matter. Even if your dog is only acting aggressively with a certain person or over a particular item, such as his food or a favorite toy, intervention is an absolute necessity. Until you have created a plan for dealing with the problem and you are seeing consistently positive results, do not allow your dog near other people.

Thinking of your dog's biting as nipping can be a slippery slope. In one of his many books about his life with dogs, Jon Katz explains that the difference between these two synonyms is arbitrary, especially to the person on the receiving end of a bite. As with the rest of the topics Katz tackles in his books, he approaches this subject with his characteristic humor, but he never pretends the problem is anything but very serious. I concur that biting of any kind is never a small problem. If your dog bites someone, you could be sued. You could even be forced to have your dog euthanized.

Even if your Springer displays no signs of aggression whatsoever, never allow him to place his teeth on your skin for any reason. Teething puppies get great satisfaction from chewing on virtually anything they can wrap their tiny chompers around, but even this seemingly innocent gnawing can set a dangerous precedent. Teach your dog that touching others with his teeth is not allowed. If you have children, make sure they too know that biting of any kind is against the rules.

If your dog acts aggressively over his food, begin hand-feeding him immediately. The old saying that a dog won't bite the hand that feeds him can be mighty accurate in a very literal sense. Offer your Springer his kibble one piece at a time, and stop immediately if you dog growls or if he takes the food from you too forcefully. If he hasn't eaten enough, you may begin hand-feeding again after a short break. Your dog will soon learn that acting aggressively means waiting for his dinner.

Chewing

Coming home to slivers of what used to be your personal property can be the fastest way to put a wedge between you and your English Springer Spaniel. Even the most tolerant owner can be upset by having precious belongings destroyed. And dogs always know when their owners are displeased with them— even though they may likely have no idea what it was they did wrong. To curb inappropriate chewing, you must remove from your dog's reach any items that could serve as impromptu toys.

If your Springer is still a puppy, expect that he will chew on virtually any item that will fit into his mouth—and even some items that won't. Chewing is a very natural canine behavior. It is even good for your Springer's jaw, teeth, and gums. So, be sure to replace the items you put away with things that your dog *should* chew. Nylabone offers a wonderful line of chewable toys in a variety of shapes and sizes.

When you cannot supervise your puppy, the best place for him is inside his crate or safety-gated into a puppy-proofed room. You cannot blame your Springer for chewing if you do not take reasonable actions to prevent it from happening. Most of this really comes down to geography. Keep temptations away from your dog, and keep him away from the temptations. For items that cannot be removed so easily, such as furniture, try applying a bitter-tasting deterrent to the item. These can be found at most pet supply stores.

A puppy's desire to chew must be redirected from your shoes or furniture to appropriate chew toys.

Do not allow your Springer to inherit items of yours he has already chewed. You may no longer have any use for these things, but giving them to your dog can send a mixed message. He won't understand why it is okay to chew this tennis shoe but not the new pair you just purchased.

When you discover your dog with something he shouldn't have, remove the item from his mouth promptly. Always offer an appropriate substitute, and praise him for accepting it. To ensure that he will accept it, make it as enticing as possible. Flavored chews can be especially appealing.

Inappropriate chewing is not a behavior exclusive to puppies. Adult Springers can also chew indiscriminately, and their larger mouths can often wreak even greater havoc on a household. Like their younger counterparts, these older dogs should also be provided with a variety of chew toys to prevent this normal activity from becoming a problem.

Digging

Digging is another very natural canine behavior, but if your English Springer Spaniel is making a compost pile of your vegetable garden, his digging has become a problem. Redirection is usually the best way to prevent a dog from digging. If your dog spends regular time alone in your backyard, provide him with plenty of toys to keep him busy. Even the most ardent diggers among this breed would rather play a game of ball with their owners than dig, but play time doesn't always have to be a joint activity. Tasty bones and balls that dispense treats can serve as excellent distractions for a dog who tends to dig most when he is bored.

If your catch your Springer in the act of digging, redirect him to another spot. Offering him a toy can help keep him from returning to the scene of the crime. Praise him for his compliance. If he continues to dig, either in the original spot or elsewhere, again move him to a different area and encourage him to participate in a new activity. If he still continues, you have two choices: Bring him indoors, or designate a small section of your yard as a dog-friendly digging zone.

Allowing your dog to dig in a small area of his own is often the most efficient way of solving this problem. True, your dog will still be digging, but by limiting him to this area, you could be saving your garden or lawn. If your Springer tries moving beyond this spot, simply redirect him back to his area, praising him for digging only there.

If providing your Springer with a place of his own in which to dig isn't an option, you may have to refrain from allowing

Another Cause of Digging

Rising temperatures can also prompt digging. Some dogs dig to create a cool rest spot on a hot day. If this is the driving force for your Springer's digging, try keeping him out of the hot sun, and always provide him with plenty of fresh drinking water.

If your Springer jumps up every time you are near, ignore him. When he sits down or lays down, only then should you dispense scratches and praise.

your dog to spend time in your yard. Most importantly, never leave your dog unattended, even with a secure fence in place. An experienced digger will often have no trouble getting out of the yard by digging a tunnel underneath the fence.

Excessive Barking

Excessive barking can be one of the most frustrating of all canine behavior problems. Not only does constant barking annoy owners, but it can also disturb their neighbors. The unwanted noise can lead to strained relationships, eviction notices, and even visits from the police.

As with many canine behavior problems, prevention is the key. Provide your English Springer Spaniel with plenty of distractions. If he tends to bark most at a certain time of day, make sure he has a fun toy to entertain him during this period. If you are usually home when he barks, take him out for a walk or an outdoor play session.

If your Springer typically barks at people walking by your home, remove his access to the windows in this area of your home, especially when you know people will be present. Use a safety gate to keep him in another room when kids will be coming home from school, for example. If he can still hear them, switch on the radio or television to muffle the sound.

Dealing with a Springer who barks virtually round the clock for can be a bit more complicated. For starters, you may not want to discourage your dog from letting you know when someone is approaching your home. Still, you don't want to listen to ongoing barking with every passerby.

In this case, you must develop of means of letting your dog know that he did a good job at alerting you, but now he must be quiet. This is when teaching the *enough* command can be extremely useful. Either wait for your Springer to begin barking, or teach him to speak on command before moving on to teaching him to stop. To teach a dog to speak, simply make some noise to elicit barking as you say the word "speak." Knocking on a door or a piece of furniture usually works well. As soon as your dog barks, reward him with a treat and praise. Eventually, your Springer will bark when you tell him to speak without your having to make any additional noise.

When you want your dog to stop barking, wait for a pause (at least a second or two), and say the word "enough," again rewarding him with both a treat and praise. You must wait for your dog to stop barking to issue the command, and the reward must be given before he returns to barking—otherwise, you will be reinforcing the wrong behavior. As you repeat this exercise, your dog will learn that the word "enough" means that he must stop barking. Be sure not to yell the command, though, since human yelling sounds a lot like barking to a dog. If you yell, he may try to join you by barking along.

Jumping Up

If your English Springer Spaniel jumps up on people when he gets excited, you must address the problem swiftly. Remember, English Springer Spaniels are so named for a reason. This breed is extremely adept at jumping. Of course, not everyone minds being jumped on by a dog, but young children and elderly adults can be hurt easily by a Springer with even the best of intentions. Also, some of your guests *will* mind being jumped on by a dog. For these reasons, it is best to correct the behavior before it has a chance to pose a problem.

When most Springers jump on people, they are seeking attention. Therefore, one of the best strategies for correcting the problem is withholding attention whenever your Springer jumps on you. As soon as your dog jumps up, interrupt him by issuing the *sit* command. When he complies, you may then show your dog some attention once again, but try to limit your animation, since your goal is to discourage him from jumping up again.

You can practice not jumping by asking a friend to help you. For the best results, select someone whom your Springer adores. When your friend arrives, instruct her to issue the *sit* command the moment your dog jumps up. Repeat this exercise several times during your friend's visit. If your Springer has a hard time reeling himself into the sitting position, you may issue the *down* command to help him control himself.

Ask your friends to never tolerate your dog's jumping. People who love animals may often say, "That's okay," and continue greeting your dog whether he's on the floor or in their faces. Explain to these well-intended friends that jumping is a problem for you and that you would really appreciate their help in solving it. When you explain that favorite friends like them are the best people to help, most will be more than willing to issue a firm "sit"—and the heartfelt praise that should always follow.

Training should not stop when your Springer is an adult.

Separation Anxiety

Most English Springer Spaniels can handle being left alone for reasonable periods of time. Spending some time alone can even be healthy for most dogs. Some Springers, however, suffer from separation anxiety, a condition in which isolation induces severe emotional distress. Dogs suffering from separation anxiety can exhibit a number of other problem behaviors, including excessive barking or howling and inappropriate chewing in response to their anxiety.

Any dog can suffer from separation

The Different Dialects of Canine Body Language

Your English Springer Spaniel's body language can reveal a lot about what he is feeling. Staring, for example, can indicate feelings of anger. Averted eyes often mean a dog is feeling fearful. Sometimes, though, the meaning behind your dog's posture is more individualized. My own dogs will stare at me when they feel it's time to go to sleep. I enjoy reading late at night, but Molly and Damon (along with my husband) prefer to go to bed early. As you get to know your Springer, you will learn what each of his movements mean. Rarely should an owner infer too much from a single gesture, though. Instead, consider your dog's entire body and attitude. When my dogs stare at me before bedtime, their teeth aren't exposed, and their bodies aren't tense, so I know they aren't angry—they're just tired.

anxiety, but it is especially common in dogs who have not been socialized properly and in dogs with neglect or abuse in their histories. Sometimes the condition can be triggered by an allergic reaction or nutritional problem.

Separation anxiety can be eased, but it takes a lot of time and patience on behalf of the dog's owner. To help prevent your Springer from suffering from this problem in the first place, socialize him as much as possible as a puppy and continue to do so as an adult. Also, avoid allowing your dog to spend all his time with you. Even if your routine involves being home with your dog most of the time, make a point of regularly leaving him home alone at least for short periods of time. This will help him understand that you sometimes leave, but you always return.

If your Springer experiences separation anxiety, talk to your veterinarian. Together you can create a plan of action. This will likely include seeking the help of a professional trainer. A wide range of strategies exist for easing the pain of separation anxiety. Training in general helps build confidence in pets, an important step in beating this form of anxiety. Medications can also be beneficial in some cases. There is even a product on the market made to mimic the pheromones of a lactating female dog, something many dogs in emotional distress find soothing.

Most importantly, never punish your dog for his separation anxiety. This will only limit your potential to correct the problem. Lessening separation anxiety involves building your Springer's trust and confidence; punishment inevitably weakens both these important characteristics.

It will take a lot of work, but puppies can be well-behaved adults.

Lifetime Training

One of the best ways to avoid problem behaviors altogether is to make training a part of your everyday life with your English Springer Spaniel. Although some owners think of training as having a well-defined finish line, the truth of the matter isn't quite so simple. Without ongoing practice, any dog can regress.

For example, each time you take your Springer out to his potty spot, praise him for eliminating. Even if you don't need him to lie down right now, practice this command (and others) whenever you have a free moment or two. This will keep the concepts fresh in your dog's mind. Like our own, we can keep our dogs' brains sharp by giving them a reason to use them. By making training a part of your everyday routine for a lifetime, you can help ensure that your dog will be open to learning new things, whenever the need arises.

How to Find an Animal Behavior Specialist

The work of an animal behaviorist involves observing, interpreting, and modifying animal behavior, so that she can help clients solve their pets' most serious problems. The biggest difference between behaviorists and other animal trainers is the severity of the problems they address. Dog trainers and obedience instructors help owners prevent negative behaviors before they become issues. They may also work with owners to correct mild behavior problems. Behaviorists, on the other hand, deal with more substantial matters.

The advice of a behaviorist may be necessary if your dog suffers from acute anxiety or phobias, aggression, or other behavioral disorders, issues with which conventional trainers are not qualified to deal. Even a veterinarian may not be able to help in many cases.

Like dog trainers and obedience instructors, behaviorists do not need any form of licensing to do their work, so careful selection is a must. Although a certification process does exist, it is still fairly new and not well known; there are currently only a limited number of certified behaviorists. You can find a directory of these individuals at www.animalbehavior.org. It is most important that you are comfortable with the individual you choose, but you should also seek a person with a certain level of education and experience dealing with animals, particularly dogs. A degree in some form of psychology or zoology is a definite advantage. The person also should possess dog-training knowledge and experience. References from former clients are good, but recommendations from veterinarians and humane societies are even better. If you cannot find a certified behaviorist on your own, these are the best resources that may lead to one.

Chapter

7

ADVANCED TRAINING and ACTIVITIES

With Your English Springer Spaniel

Participating in advanced training activities can be enormously rewarding for both English Springer Spaniels and their owners. Whether you choose to show your Springer in conformation events or enter your dog in obedience trials, an organized activity is a great way to meet other people who share a common interest: dogs. Many Springer owners told me that some of their best friends are fellow dog lovers, and this is no coincidence, for a great number of owners have met through clubs and other organizations that sponsor events of this kind.

An organized activity is also a great way to allow your Springer to develop his individual talents. Perhaps your dog has remarkable balance. He just might be a future agility champion waiting to earn his first title. Maybe your Springer learns new commands with amazing ease. How do you know if he's ready to take his skills to the next level—say, in formal obedience competitions?

If you are unsure if a particular activity is right for you or your Springer, start by practicing right in your own backyard. Then consider enrolling in a beginner-level obedience class or attending an agility event as a spectator. If you enjoy it, and your dog seems to take to it, dig a little deeper. Buy a small piece of agility equipment for your backyard, or create your own. A child's play tunnel can easily double as an agility tunnel until you are certain your dog is a good match for the sport.

Just like kids, most dogs relish opportunities to learn new things and show off their newly discovered skills. Likewise, they can benefit in numerous ways. A dog who takes part in regular organized events will likely become more social, more cooperative and self-confident, and even a lot happier. There's nothing quite like that feeling of purpose and belonging that participating in an organized activity offers.

CANINE GOOD CITIZEN® PROGRAM

One of the best platforms for any advanced training activity—and truly an accomplishment within itself—is the completion of the American Kennel Club's (AKC)

Canine Good Citizen (CGC) program. A certification series begun in 1989, the CGC program stresses responsible pet ownership by rewarding dogs who display good manners both at home and in the community. Those interested may attend the CGC training program, an optional class offered to owners and their dogs, before taking a very detailed ten-step test. Upon completion, certificates are awarded.

The CGC program focuses primarily on a dog's obedience skills and temperament, but it also stresses the importance of serious owner commitment. All owners are required to sign a *Responsible Dog Owners Pledge* before taking the test. This unique document states that the owner agrees to effectively care for her dog for the rest of the animal's life. It also encompasses such important areas as health and safety, exercise and training, and basic quality of life. It even addresses such community-based issues as agreeing to clean up after your pet in public and never allowing your dog to infringe on the rights of others.

A dog who passes this valuable examination is awarded an AKC certificate complete with the CGC logo embossed in gold.

Graduating from the American Kennel Club's Canine Good Citizen (CGC) program is a great beginning if you'd like your Springer to become a therapy dog.

CGC certification can also be useful to your dog in many other areas of advanced training. A dog worthy of the revered title of Canine Good Citizen is considered a responsible member of his community, a community that includes both people and dogs that he already knows and all of those he will encounter in the future. Although dogs of any age may participate in the CGC program, puppies must be at least old enough to have had all necessary immunizations. To ensure that your dog's certification is reliable, it is strongly recommended that younger dogs who pass the test get retested as adults, since temperaments and abilities may change during this formative period. All breeds (as well as mixed breeds) are welcome in the program.

GAMES AND TRICKS

Owners needn't fill out a single registration form to spend quality time with their English Springer Spaniels. Sometimes the best playtime is the informal kind. Most Springers love chasing balls, playing fetch, and just running around with their favorite people and other dogs. And play time certainly isn't limited to these more traditional canine games. Many Springers also enjoy playing hide and seek and follow the leader. Some owners make up games to play with their dogs—like doggy basketball. All you need is a ball your Springer can grasp with his mouth and a makeshift hoop—a couple of tires stacked together or even a large bucket will suffice.

One of the benefits of this unstructured time with your pet is that it allows you to think outside the doghouse. Maybe your Springer loves learning new tricks, but the two of you have exhausted all the conventional favorites like shaking hands and rolling over. Perhaps you could teach your dog to wave or jump rope. Some owners teach their Springers to pick up their toys and put them away—a trick with a dual purpose.

Watch your dog for clues to what he enjoys doing most. Some Springers like to be challenged mentally. A great variation of hide and seek is hiding a toy instead of yourself. Other Springers take great pleasure in being vocal; a dog like this can

Does My Springer Need Off-Leash Time?

Many owners feel strongly that dogs should never be allowed off their leads in unfenced areas, period. Additionally, most municipalities have firm leash laws in place for a good reason. Keeping your dog leashed keeps him safe. Automobiles and wild animals pose the biggest threats to pets, but an unleashed dog can also become lost, leaving him vulnerable to the elements and a host of other dangers. Leashes also protect people from being jumped on or bitten by dogs prone to these behaviors.

Still, a good number of dog lovers tout the benefits of regular off-leash playtime in areas where it is allowed by law. Owners who let their dogs run freely insist that their dogs are better adjusted, more social, and even less aggressive than their tethered canine counterparts. Fortunately, many communities now have dog parks—fenced areas where dogs can meet and run free. These canine playgrounds provide many dogs with the best of both worlds. But not all areas have dog parks. If yours does not, should you travel to a more rural location for off-lead recreation?

The biggest problem with taking your Springer to a more remote area for off-leash time is that, with a more secluded location, there comes a greater likelihood that one of you will become lost or encounter wildlife. If your dog has not been trained to obey your commands in this setting, you must be extremely careful when deciding to remove that leash. Your decision could cost your dog his life.

NYLABONE

The active nature of the Springer breed is perfect for the many games and tricks you can play with and teach your dog.

be taught to sing along to music. My Spaniel Molly serenades my husband and me several mornings each week before we even climb out of bed. Because of her fondness for toy pigs, we pretend that Molly is the lead singer for a wacky rock band called Twisted Piggy. If this seems silly, that's the whole point! Play should always be fun for everyone involved. Molly delights in hearing our praise whenever she composes a new song for us.

Making time for this type of play is far more important than what you choose to do with your Springer. Even if your dog is involved in an organized activity, he can benefit greatly from having some free time with you, as well. Your Springer may be the most dedicated hunting companion or flyball competitor in the world, but never underestimate the value in allowing him—at least once in a while—to just be a dog.

OBEDIENCE

For many dog owners, advanced training in obedience begins with a relatively casual level of involvement—taking your English Springer Spaniel to a basic obedience class as a puppy, for instance. You may even decide to check out competitive obedience after working with your dog privately to teach him a few commands you think he should know. In many cases though, both dog and owner discover that this seemingly stoic style of training can actually be a really fun pastime for all involved. Advanced obedience training, when properly implemented, is simply higher education for your Springer.

In obedience competition, the first class you will enter is the novice class, also called the Companion Dog (CD) class. This beginning level focuses on demonstrating the skills of a good canine companion—heeling both on and off the leash at different speeds, coming when called, and staying for fixed periods of time while also remaining still and quiet with a group of other dogs. Your Springer will also be required to stand for a basic physical examination by the judges.

Next comes the open class. This second tier of obedience is also called the Companion Dog Excellent (CDX) class. At this level, your dog will need to repeat many of the same exercises from the novice level, but off leash and for longer periods of time. Jumping and retrieving tasks are also included in this phase.

The utility level, which provides your Springer with a Utility Dog (UD) title, is for dogs nearing the top of their obedience game. At this stage, your dog will need to perform more difficult exercises, complete with hand signals, as well as scent

Everything in Moderation

With their deep chests and large lungs, English Springer Spaniels seem to be built for activity. In most cases, the typical daily walk is not enough to keep this breed properly conditioned. Still, owners must be sure their dogs aren't overdoing it. For Springers who are still growing, it is especially important that exercise be limited to reasonable amounts and levels of intensity. A brisk, 30-minute walk usually provides an adequate workout. Hiking and swimming are also acceptable pastimes for this active breed. Jogging or running alongside an owner riding a bicycle, however, can destroy a young Springer's joints. Taking your Springer to a dog park where he can run around at his own pace is ideal. Playing fetch can be great exercise for this breed, providing you watch your dog carefully for signs that he's tiring. Older dogs tend to tire more quickly than younger ones, and seniors can overexert themselves sometimes. Springers have such an intense urge to please their owners that they will often push themselves beyond their need for rest. As your dog's owner, it is your job to make sure his activities are appropriate for both his age and activity level.

discrimination tasks. Once your dog can perform at this level, he can then go on to pursue the highest possible titles of Obedience Trial Champion (OTCh) and Utility Dog Excellent (UDX). Both are very prestigious titles and not easily nor quickly achieved.

Like the CGC program, obedience is considered by many Springer enthusiasts to be a great foundation for many other canine activities. Maybe your ultimate plan is for your dog to become a therapy dog, or perhaps you just want to participate in a fun weekend pastime together, with awards being just an added bonus. No matter what obedience means to you and your dog, bear in mind that succeeding does not mean that your dog must earn all available titles. As with any activity, there is nothing wrong with striving toward your next goal, but the most important thing is enjoying the road that leads there. Any owner of an English Springer Spaniel who earns a CDX or UD title should be very proud, as these are very reputable accomplishments.

SHOWING YOUR ENGLISH SPRINGER SPANIEL

Dog shows, also called conformation events, evaluate just how closely the entrants match their breed's standard, an indication of an animal's ability to produce quality puppies. Because showing began as a means of evaluating breeding stock, spayed and neutered dogs may not participate. A member of the AKC's sporting group, the English Springer Spaniel is no

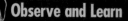

Observe and Learn

If you are in the process of selecting an obedience instructor, ask each trainer you are considering if you may observe a class before committing to a program. This will show you each person's individual style and methods. Be sure to sit in on a puppy or beginner class though, as this will provide you with the most basic example of how the instructor tackles the training process.

Watch how the trainer interacts with each dog and owner. Obedience instructors should possess a genuine love for dogs, and they should also communicate with owners easily. The advice the instructor offers should be clear and easy for owners to follow. And it should never include punishment of any kind. Look for a trainer who understands that each dog is different and may require a slightly altered approach.

If an instructor promises lightning-fast results, consider this a huge warning sign. Remember, obedience training can be a lengthy process—especially if you plan to involve your English Springer Spaniel in obedience trials. Look for an instructor who seems to understand that slow and steady wins the race. Every command learned builds on the previous training task. When it comes to dog training, successfully teaching your Springer puppy to sit or lie down is an accomplishment worth celebrating. A good trainer will share in an owner's enthusiasm for reaching these early goals.

Dress For Success

It's easy to overdress for the conformation ring. Of course, you want to look your best when showing your English Springer Spaniel, but how dressy should you go? Judges frequently don the fanciest clothes when overseeing large-scale events. At first you may feel underdressed—or even disrespectful—by not matching their level of dress. It's important to understand, however that handlers are not expected to dress so elaborately. Judges understand that handlers must do a lot of running around while showing their dogs. This can make many dresses and high-heeled shoes poor choices for female handlers. For women, the best options are usually pantsuits or split skirts paired with flat shoes. Men frequently wear khakis and sport coats in the ring. Certainly, jeans and sneakers are too casual, but be sure whatever clothes you choose fit comfortably and allow you to move with ease. When in doubt, go with something simple. Remember, your dog should be the one to stand out. Avoid flashy colors or anything else that might distract the judges from your beautiful English Springer Spaniel.

stranger to the ring. The breed has been formally shown in the United States for more than a century.

Before a Springer, or any breed for that matter, can be entered into a conformation show, he must meet certain criteria. A complete list of rules and regulations governing eligibility may be obtained from the AKC, but basic guidelines require that your dog be a purebred English Springer Spaniel, AKC-registered, and at least six months old. Show dogs cannot have registration papers that limit their breeding, but a breeder may change a limited dog's status by making a written request to the AKC.

How Dog Shows Work

Shows can range in size and variety from small, local specialty events to national all-breed shows with more than 3,000 entrants. Even if you have no plans of ever showing your Springer, attending a large-scale AKC conformation event can be an amazing experience for any true dog fancier. At no other place will you ever see so many different breeds all in one place, many of which you may have never seen previously.

Breeds are divided into seven groups: sporting dogs, hounds, working dogs, terriers, toys, nonsporting dogs, and herding dogs. Each dog is then placed in one of five classes: puppy, novice, bred by exhibitor, American-bred, and open. Males are always judged first. Once an English Springer Spaniel is judged best of breed, that dog then goes on to represent his breed in the group competition.

From a novice perspective, it may seem that many of the dogs belonging to each breed look nearly identical. To the well-trained eye of an AKC judge, however, the differences can be significant. Judges look at every nuance of an individual dog to compare him to his breed standard. All entrants are carefully scrutinized in this way, and those dogs with obvious faults are eliminated, allowing the best specimens to rise to the top of the competition.

Dogs accumulate between one and five points with each win. The number of points awarded depends on the number of dogs in competition, the location of the event, and several other factors. Shows awarding three or more points are considered majors. A total of 15 points is necessary for championship status. When a dog reaches this level, he has earned the title of Champion (abbreviated as "Ch.") to be used before his name thereafter.

The English Springer Spaniel is a beautiful breed, one that has won several conformation events.

Getting Started

If you are interested in participating in conformation events, begin by first attending shows as a spectator. If the grooming area is open to the public, introduce yourself to the other English Springer Spaniel owners there, and ask if they would mind telling you about their experiences with showing. Although this is a competitive environment, many extremely kind and outgoing people are involved in the activity who are willing to help newcomers and who also enjoy sharing their enthusiasm for the breed with other kindred spirits.

In addition to exhibitors, vendors and information booths can also be valuable resources. If you are still considering purchasing your first

English Springer Spaniel, these are all wonderful starting points. Most of the breeders at AKC-sanctioned events are among the very best and can help point you toward a show-quality dog if this is what you are seeking.

If you have already purchased your dog, consider joining your local English Springer Spaniel club. You will likely find that the organization offers classes for conformation training. Entering this sport and absorbing all the necessary information can be overwhelming. By taking it slowly and learning as much as you can, you will help ensure a positive experience for both you and your dog.

Like other advanced training activities, showing requires great discipline on behalf of both dog and handler, but many people involved find it to be a labor of love. Showing English Springer Spaniels can serve as a gateway to endless learning about this breed, wonderful friends who share your affinity for Springers, and an opportunity to strengthen your bond with your special pet.

Showing in the U.S. and England

Although the showing process in Great Britain's Kennel Club (KC) is relatively similar to that in the AKC, the road to championship there is considerably different. In England, there is no point system. Instead, judges award dogs with Challenge Certificates. It is left up to the judge to decide how many dogs are worthy of this honor, so the overall number of entrants is somewhat irrelevant.

Show Business

You may think your English Springer Spaniel is perfect for conformation, but you must carefully consider whether showing is right for your dog before entering him in competition. Only Springers who match the breed standard extremely closely fair well in the show ring. Perhaps your dog has the quintessential Springer stance. If he has a bad bite—just one or two teeth out of place—he will be faulted for this inadequacy. Maybe your dog fits the physical description of an English Springer Spaniel, but he gets nervous around large groups of people and other dogs. A Springer's good temperament is as much a part of his success in the ring as any physical attribute.

If you are interested in participating in conformation, tell your breeder that you are looking for a show-quality Springer. No breeder can promise show success of course, but an experienced one can help steer you toward a puppy with the most potential in this area. Most dogs destined for the show ring are the offspring of previous champions, but even a fancy pedigree is no guarantee.

If the Springer you choose turns out to be better suited for another activity, such as therapy work or agility, consider getting involved in that pastime instead. Sometimes our dogs help us discover new and wonderful hobbies we never realized we'd enjoy so much. Most importantly, always appreciate your Springer for his individual talents. A show judge may see only your dog's faults, but you can see all his potential as a mighty worthy companion.

Not every Springer is show quality, but that doesn't mean your dog isn't a wonderful pet—far from it!

Competition can be fierce, however, with shows often extending over several days each.

To obtain championship status, a dog must receive three Challenge Certificates from three different judges. One of these certificates must be awarded after the dog is 12 months old.

For many years, criticism has been made that Challenge Certificates were being given out far too often, and that less than completely deserving dogs have received them. As a means of ensuring proper understanding of the criteria, the Kennel Club General Committee changed the wording of the official regulations for this award, effective January 1, 2005.

Another difference is the focused area of expertise of English judges compared to American judges. In England, judges who specialize in one particular breed are far more common. Since they have had such vast experience with the dogs they breed (or have bred in the past), these judges are considered the best authorities on that breed by the KC. An AKC judge is much more likely to judge several different breeds, having accumulated knowledge of them all without necessarily breeding all of them personally.

SPORTS

Many English Springer Spaniel owners enjoy being as active as their athletic pets. Canine sports offer these dog owners the opportunity to share in both the fun and exercise of advanced training activities. If you've never led an energetic Springer around an agility course, you simply don't know what you are missing. Like trying new things? Consider trying flyball or canine freestyle with your dog. These canine sports are much more entertaining than sitting through a spinning class, and what's more, they allow you to spend fun time with your best friend.

Agility

An excellent opportunity for combining exercise and mental stimulation, agility is also a truly interactive sport. Although the sport of agility has only been recognized here in the United States since 1994, it was actually developed in England back in the 1970s. Resembling equestrian jumping competitions, canine agility courses consist of similar obstacles, but they are built to a smaller scale.

One thing that certainly isn't downsized, however, is the fun. Agility competitions have quickly become an amazingly popular pastime in this country, for both participants and a mass of mesmerized onlookers. As handlers run alongside their dogs, the canine athletes make their way over colorful bars, vaulted walks, and seesaws. Keep watching, and you will see the same dogs dash through A-frames, suspended tires, and tunnels. Handlers may assist their pups by offering hand signals, verbal commands, or both.

If your energetic Springer puppy seems destined for this activity, you will have a few months to attend some events and work with your dog informally before making a final decision. Unlike obedience, a dog must be 12 months old to compete in agility. Although dogs must be physically fit for either activity, agility is considerably more strenuous on your dog's body than obedience. Because a puppy's growing bones and ligaments are weaker than an adult's, the potential for injury is lessened substantially by waiting this reasonable amount of time.

You can, of course, start introducing your dog to agility obstacles at any age. Encouraging a young dog to run through chutes or tunnels, for instance, may very well help him avoid any fears of these objects later. Avoid any tasks involving jumping, however, until your dog is older. If you would like to at least familiarize your puppy with bar jumps, you may simple lay one bar on the ground and have your dog walk over it instead of jumping over it.

Double Duty

You may wonder if an English Springer Spaniel bred for hunting can be shown in conformation events and vice versa. The technical answer is yes. No rules bar field dogs from competing in conformation shows, nor a show dog from entering field trials. However, this is not a common scenario. Springer breeders who raise dogs for hunting have very different objectives than those striving for show qualities. Neither Springer is better than the other, but it can be very difficult for a field-type Springer to match the breed standard closely enough to advance in the show ring, and most show dogs lack the physical structure and instinct necessary to become adept hunters.

Agility is a fun sport that includes obstacles like balancing boards and tunnels. Just be sure not to push your dog too hard!

All dog breeds (and mixes) are welcome to participate in agility. This is ultimately where the similarities of agility and obedience end, though. One distinctive difference that many agility enthusiasts tout as an advantage of their pastime is the amount of handler involvement allowed in this sport. Agility handlers are permitted to talk to their dogs, redirect them verbally, or cheer them on at any time.

Setup and Equipment

Every activity has both advantages as well as disadvantages. In the case of agility, the biggest drawbacks are the cost of setup and the space required for the multiple pieces of equipment. It can also be relatively time-consuming to assemble a backyard course for practice, especially if you need to disassemble it when you are finished so that the space can be used for something else.

In some areas, owners who don't have the resources to practice the sport at home can rent entire agility rings by the hour or the day. In the beginning, you can also use certain makeshift items in place of more expensive equipment. For example, a home extension ladder can help teach a dog to walk within a narrow space or train him to focus his attention forward. Once you have determined that your Springer is well suited to agility, you should then make a point of transitioning to conventional equipment so that your dog can acclimate to any subtle changes that could make a difference in his future performance in the ring. Any item you use should also be completely safe for your dog.

Once ready for competition, your Springer will be entered in the novice class. Succeeding at this level will earn your dog a Novice Agility Dog (NAD) title. Subsequent titles are then available in the following order: Open Agility Dog (OAD), Agility Dog Excellent (ADX), and Master Agility Excellent (MAX). In order to obtain each title, a dog must earn a qualifying score in the respective class on three separate occasions and from two different judges. Issuance of the MAX title is dependent upon ten qualifying scores in the Agility Excellent Class.

Canine Freestyle

If you and your English Springer Spaniel enjoy moving around to music, musical freestyle may be just the sport to provide both you and your pet with a fun opportunity for exercise and entertainment. Lead by the World Canine Freestyle Organization (WCFO), this sport is relatively new, but it has been catching on all over the world for the last couple of decades. There are two basic varieties of freestyle—musical freestyle and heelwork-to-music. The former version consists of carefully choreographed music programs in which both the owner and dog dance together. It involves intense teamwork, athleticism, and even costumes for both participants. The latter version incorporates traditional canine obedience skills into the routine. Both require an intense level of creativity and a willingness to let loose and have fun.

Although freestyle is very much a form of individual artistic expression, rules dictate what is and isn't allowed in competition. Likewise, a very specific point system is followed for judging. A 35-page list of these guidelines is available at the WCFO's website, www.worldcaninefreestyle.org.

Freestyle is truly an event for the whole family. An owner may compete in canine freestyle with either one or two dogs. Two people may compete together with their canine duo in a pairs event, or participants may compete together in teams of three or more people and an equal number of dogs. There is also a junior division for kids under 18 years of age and dogs under

The Gift of Purpose

Like people, most dogs delight in participating in fun and rewarding activities. There is a big difference between merely passing time and spending time with a purpose. Dogs find fulfillment in many of the same ways as people. They enjoy learning new things, getting exercise, and being with those they love. Organized activities like obedience and agility provide excellent opportunities for English Springer Spaniels to spend their time productively. Participating in a sport also offers regular mental stimulation and socialization. One of the best gifts you can give your Springer is a meaningful way to spend each day.

Background Players

Some dogs and their owners prefer quieter sports. Maybe a competitive environment takes the fun away from organized activities for you. Or perhaps your English Springer Spaniel prefers getting his exercise without the pressure to perform in front of an audience. If this is the case, you can still take part in many great outdoor activities together.

By taking your Springer hiking, you can both get an effective workout and explore the state in which you live. The best thing about hiking is that you can set the pace and distance that's right for you. Don't forget to bring along plenty of fresh drinking water for both you and your pet, even for a short hike. Your Springer can even carry his water (and some food, if it will be a long hike) in a canine backpack.

If you enjoy swimming, you couldn't ask for a better partner than a Springer to accompany you for a dip. For added fun, bring along a buoyant toy for your dog to retrieve from the water. You can play fetch with him from the beach when you need a break. Many Springers even enjoy riding in kayaks with their owners. Just be sure to pick up a life jacket made specifically for your canine passenger. Springers are excellent swimmers, but every member (both human and canine) of your kayaking party should wear a proper flotation device at all times in case of an emergency.

six months, as well as a senior division for people 65 and older and dogs nine years and up. There is even a division for mentally and/or physically handicapped dogs and their owners who also may be mentally and/or challenged.

The best way to learn about canine freestyle is by attending an event. Many offer instruction workshops for those interested in becoming involved in this fun new sport.

Like the recent inclusion of ice dancing in the Winter Olympics, acceptance of canine freestyle as a bona fide sport among dog enthusiasts is still in its early stages. Many owners who prefer more traditional sports such as flyball or agility may scoff at dogs and owners jitter-bugging their way across the dance ring, but it's clearly those participants who are having the most fun. Watching a freestyle competition can be great fun for onlookers as well. You will be truly amazed at what some of these dogs and their owners can do.

Flyball

Flyball is an exciting canine sport that requires both speed and dexterity. Upon hearing a signal, the dog's owner releases him on the flyball course, a small and straight strip of land. His goal is to run over four hurdles to the end of this course, where a box with a trap and foot lever awaits him. The dog then jumps onto the foot lever, releasing a tennis ball into the air. After he leaps to catch this ball, he then darts back to his owner with the ball. This is all timed down to the second. Typically, flyball is a team sport, consisting of two to four relay teams of four dogs per team. Dogs may compete on either single-breed or multi-breed teams.

Flyball is a particularly fun pastime for dogs ready to take regular ball playing to the next level. A great number of dogs competing in flyball are members of the herding group, but all breeds (and even mixed breeds) are allowed to play on multi-breed teams. Many Springers can give even the fastest Border Collie a run for his money at this fast-paced canine sport.

Hunting and Field Trials

If your English Springer Spaniel has retained the breed's

Springers are excellent dogs for hunters.

love of the hunt, field trials may offer him an exciting opportunity to get back to his roots. Styled after traditional game hunts, these exciting events provide a unique chance for owners and dogs to compete together in this oldest canine sport. An individual event may be open to multiple sporting breeds or limited to just one. Championship points are only issued in the latter case, however.

Certainly, Springers can still hunt in the old-fashioned way. The purpose of field trial clubs is to prepare sporting dogs for either activity, so a dog trained through one of these organizations should be capable of vying for titles and putting food on his owners' table.

If you think you might enjoy competing in this sport with your Springer, get him involved when he is as young as possible. You can have a puppy tested for so-called "birdiness"

A visit from a therapy dog is a wonderful and rewarding experience for you, your dog, and the patients you visit.

before deciding if this is the dog for you. Many kennels breed with this hunting purpose in mind; you will probably have the best luck finding a Springer well suited to this activity by purchasing a dog from one of these breeders. An English Springer Spaniel can start training as early as just eight weeks old. It is not unusual to see a pup this age training alongside an older, more seasoned counterpart, each carrying a wing as they proudly retrieve a bird together.

Like formal obedience trials, field trials offer several levels of competition with a respective point system for each, but the specifics are a bit more complicated for this activity. The number of other breeds involved in a particular event and even an individual dog's age, for example, can play important roles. A good breeder experienced in this sport should be able to help guide you through the process.

THERAPY WORK

At the end of a bad day, I am always especially grateful to have my dogs by my side. Even if nothing else has gone right, they make me laugh and remind me not to take life too seriously. If I'm feeling ill, they remain steadfastly by my side, getting my mind off whatever is ailing me. They even make good days all that much better. I'm sure many of you can relate to these scenarios, as almost all dogs offer a similar boost for their beloved owners.

An American nurse named Elaine Smith took this means of raising a dog lover's spirits to a whole new level. While working in England, Smith noticed the positive effect pets had on patients when they visited them alongside human friends and volunteers. These interactions were the inspiration for the organization Smith founded when she returned to the United States in the late 1970s—Therapy Dogs International, Inc., or TDI.

For decades, studies have shown that Smith's observations went far beyond merely elevating a patient's mood, a worthy effort in itself. For people who love dogs, sometimes just being around this unique species is enough to stimulate physiological changes in their health. Very real changes in mental health also have been observed.

A recent study by the University of California Los Angeles Medical Center revealed that anxiety in heart failure patients dropped an astounding 24 percent when visited by a volunteer with a therapy dog. Another group of heart patients who were visited by a human volunteer alone experienced only a 10-percent drop. No change was noted in patients not visited. The data on epinephrine levels of patients receiving therapy dog visits was also significant. This stress hormone dropped about 17 percent in those who spent time with a volunteer and therapy dog, but the decrease was only 2 percent in those visited by the volunteer alone. And patients who received no visits? Their stress levels increased by about 7 percent.

Dogs of any breed, as well as mixed breeds, can be therapy dogs. Perhaps you think your English Springer Spaniel has what it takes to be one. Many Springers indeed perform this important and rewarding work. The 2007 Westminster Best in Show winner Ch. Felicity's Diamond Jim is better known to many of his friends as James, the certified therapy dog.

Certification begins with a test by a TDI evaluator. A dog must be at least a year old at this time and possess a sound temperament. Passing the AKC's Canine Good Citizen test is also a prerequisite. A potential therapy dog's behavior is observed around both people and service equipment, such as crutches and wheelchairs. A health record form must be completed by the dog's veterinarian as well. Like a doctor's, a therapy dog's first responsibility is to do no harm to the patients he visits. For more information, please visit TDI's website at www.tdi-dog.org.

Pet Therapy

Therapy pets are often used in health care, social, educational, and recreational settings. In health care, therapy pets help facilitate physical and psychological sessions with patients of all ages, whether a psychological counseling session in which a patient feels free to speak with an animal in the room, or a round of physical therapy in which the patient is encouraged to groom or walk a pet.

Among older Americans, therapy animals can be used in hospices, nursing homes, hospitals, short-term care facilities, and even residential dwellings to facilitate therapeutic interaction. Therapy animals visit patients, who are encouraged to pet, interact, and play with them. These interactions often result in the improved physical health and mental well-being of the patient.

But the benefits of pet therapy can work both ways. The people who provide pet therapy services often speak about how rewarding it is for them. Even better, pets and people of any age can volunteer in a therapeutic capacity. Some organizations even prefer to provide pet therapy to senior citizens using older pets—further proof that age doesn't matter when love is involved.

(Courtesy of the Humane Society of the United States)

HEALTH

of Your English Springer Spaniel

Keeping your English Springer Spaniel healthy is one of the most important jobs you will ever perform as a pet owner. It is also one of the most diverse, for good health comes from staying on top of tasks in many areas of his life. Sound nutrition, adequate exercise, and even regular grooming play important roles in this process. Being proactive about veterinary care is another smart step. Certainly, your dog's veterinarian is there to help you deal with any illnesses or injuries as they occur, but she can help you prevent many health problems as well.

FINDING A VET

At one time, finding a veterinarian for your dog meant asking a pet-owning neighbor for the name of the local vet when you moved to a new town. Today, you have many more choices. Perhaps you want a veterinarian trained in alternative therapies, such as homeopathy or acupuncture. Or you may want a hospital that offers separate waiting areas for sick patients and those visiting for routine exams. Whatever your personal preferences, you are likely to find just the right vet for you and your English Springer Spaniel, providing you take a little time to do your homework.

Recommendations

Interestingly, that old word-of-mouth method for finding a veterinarian still works well. Ask your neighbors—and your other friends and family members—which veterinarians they use. Even more importantly, ask each person why she uses this particular vet. A happy client will usually bubble over with praise and anecdotes.

You may also ask your local humane society for the names of veterinarians in your area whom they recommend. Of course, you can find these names in your local telephone book, but having the recommendation of an organization like this can help you decide where to start your search—especially with the list of vets in most areas growing so rapidly.

Do Your Research

Once you have found a veterinarian you would like to consider, get online. Check out the hospital's website (most have one these days), and read up on its policies. This can save you a lot of time in the interviewing process. Look for the hours of operation, costs of routine services, and location. Although these aren't the most important factors when selecting a doctor, they can certainly have an impact on both you and your pet. If a hospital is only open when you are at work, for example, its vets can be the very best available, and your Springer still won't be able to benefit from their expertise. Likewise, if a vet's prices would stress your budget, it could make it difficult for you to properly care for your dog if he faces a serious issue.

If a veterinarian is located farther away than you would like to travel, you may certainly continue your search, but this is one obstacle that may be worth dealing with if you think the vet is worth it. The inconvenience of traveling an extra 20 minutes for

You should feel comfortable with your veterinarian and trust her completely with the well-being of your dog.

an annual exam pales in comparison to giving your dog the best available veterinary care. If you choose a vet located more than 30 minutes away, though, be sure to familiarize yourself with an emergency clinic closer to home.

Emergency Veterinary Clinics

Most emergency clinics are open when conventional veterinary hospitals are closed. Some, however, remain open even during typical business hours. Check with your local emergency clinic to see what hours it keeps. If you bring your Springer to the hospital only to find it closed, valuable time will be wasted.

It is wise to scope out an emergency hospital even if your regular veterinarian is within a reasonable distance to your home. Use reasonable judgment when deciding which situations warrant this type of care, though. Most emergency clinics charge a lot more than conventional veterinary hospitals. Also, emergency vets are there to treat true emergencies. Much like an emergency room for people, emergency clinics must triage their patients, meaning they treat animals with life-threatening emergencies first. If your dog's problem can wait until your regular vet can see him, this is the better choice.

Interviewing a Potential Vet

Whether you are selecting a conventional veterinary hospital or an emergency clinic, visiting the facility before your Springer needs to be seen is a wise step. Before choosing a particular hospital, schedule a tour, and be sure to bring your Springer with you. Most vets welcome visits of this kind (beware of any that don't), but you must be respectful of the hospital's schedule. Most vets perform surgeries early in the morning. Midday can also be a busy time, since working pet owners frequently try to squeeze appointments into their lunch hours. Late afternoon is usually the best time for the staff to show you around and answer your questions about the hospital. Similarly, Mondays and Fridays may be busier than other weekdays. When minor problems strike on weekends, many owners wait until Monday to bring their dogs to the vet. Likewise, Friday is a popular day for clients to ask to be fit into a hospital's

Don't Be Fooled

Don't be fooled by large waiting rooms and fancy equipment. The biggest act in town isn't always the best. You will pay more for appointments at these more extravagant hospitals, so be sure the care they offer is up to par.

schedule, since owners want to make sure that a smaller problem doesn't become more serious over the weekend when the hospital is closed and the only other option is the emergency clinic.

Drop by Unannounced

Dropping by unannounced during a busy time to schedule your tour, however, is a shrewd move. Doing so can give you a sneak peek of how things work on a day-to-day basis. Is the hospital clean? Are there enough staff members to handle the patients? Do the other dog owners seem pleased with their pets' care? Remember, your Springer won't be dealing with just the veterinarian; he will also interact with the veterinary technicians and other staff members. Each person should possess an obvious love for animals and a positive attitude.

Ask Questions

Ask as many questions as possible during your tour, and listen carefully to the answers. If several veterinarians are on staff, ask if your dog will be seen by the same doctor for each appointment—a plus. Many dogs, especially those who balk at the idea of going to a vet in the first place, do better when they are able to establish a rapport with a specific vet. Ask about the protocol for referring clients in the event that a dog's needs surpass the expertise of the hospital's staff. Beware of any veterinarian who claims that she can treat any condition. A good doctor knows her limitations. While she may indeed be able to handle most situations, she should always be willing to refer patients to another doctor if doing so would be best for the dog. Likewise, if the vet doesn't have the answer to one of your questions, she should be willing to find the answer for you— and explain it in simple terms without condescension. You and the vet you choose will be partners in your Springer's care; this should be a mutually respectful relationship.

Watch Your Dog's Reactions

Watch your Springer carefully throughout the tour. How does he respond to the vet and other employees? Smart vets offer healthy treats as a way of showing dogs that visiting the vet can be fun. Once you choose a hospital, stop by occasionally for a treat and attention when you are in the neighborhood. If the only time your dog sees the vet is when he must be examined, he will more likely become uneasy at the sight (and smell) of the hospital.

Finally, heed your own instincts. If you feel uneasy with a particular vet or hospital, keep looking. Extensive experience and clean, organized facilities should rank high on your list of priorities, but even these important qualities can't take the place of finding a veterinarian you trust.

PHYSICAL EXAMINATIONS

A healthy English Springer Spaniel won't need to see his

A quality veterinarian's office will be clean, the help will be friendly and knowledgeable, and the doctor will care as much about your dog as you do.

veterinarian often, but an owner should never underestimate the importance of routine care. If your dog appears to be in good physical shape, you may think there is little harm in skipping an exam. Just because your dog looks healthy, though, doesn't mean he is healthy. Missing a single appointment can mean missing the earliest signs of a serious medical issue—signs that only a vet may notice.

In the wild, sick dogs are often expelled from their packs, left to fend for themselves. Many die when this happens. Both wild and domesticated dogs hide their symptoms out of a natural instinct to mask illness for this reason. Also, many illnesses present no symptoms whatsoever until the disease has progressed to a dangerous stage. Remember, when cared for properly, most English Springer Spaniels have a lifespan of between 12 and 14 years or more.

Regular visits to the vet not only provide your Springer with the medical care he needs, but they also offer you an opportunity to ask the vet any questions you may have about your dog's care. These may relate to health issues, training topics, or even feeding and grooming concerns. Your veterinarian should always be your first resource for gathering information about caring for your pet.

First Checkup

Your Springer's initial checkup sets an important precedent. This important appointment introduces your dog to the world of veterinary care. A positive first experience can make all the difference in how he reacts to future visits. Likewise, a stressful encounter can cause both you and your dog to dread upcoming vet visits.

Most importantly, don't rush through this first exam. Allow staff members to play with your dog and lavish him with attention. This will show him that the veterinary hospital can be a fun place. If you maintain a fun attitude, your puppy will likely follow your lead.

Once you have filled out all the necessary paperwork, a veterinary technician will lead you to a private room and begin your dog's exam by weighing him and taking his temperature. The vet will then arrive and check your dog for any physical abnormalities. She will examine his eyes, ears, and teeth. She will feel his abdomen for any enlarged organs and check his legs for any loose joints. She will also listen to his heart and lungs with a stethoscope.

Answer any questions the vet or technicians ask you as fully as possible. This first appointment is largely about information gathering, so your vet can provide your dog with the best possible care. If you are worried that you may forget some of your own questions, write them down ahead of time, and don't be afraid to ask anything at all. Learning as much as you can about your Springer's care makes you a good owner. Most vet offices will answer questions that may come up later over the phone, but

Do the Right Thing

Even if your English Springer Spaniel is still just weeks old, talk to your vet about your plans for spaying or neutering your dog at your very first visit. You can even make an appointment right then and there. Unless you will be showing or breeding your Springer, sterilization should be done sooner rather than later. Evidence has shown that spaying a female dog before her first heat cycle drastically reduces her chances of getting breast cancer. By having your male Springer neutered, you effectively eliminate his risk for testicular cancer and also considerably reduce his chances of getting prostate cancer. Sterilization, commonly called "fixing" an animal, also offers other perks, such as less mess (without heat), fewer behavioral problems (including marking and aggression), and a decreased desire to roam the neighborhood in search of female dogs.

An English Springer Spaniel may be spayed or neutered as early as four months of age. This simple operation is performed by veterinarians every day. In addition to helping to keep your dog healthy, sterilization also helps control the unwanted pet population—a number that is currently in the millions worldwide.

the best time to address any concerns you have is during your dog's visits.

Vaccination Schedule

Your breeder will have begun your English Springer Spaniel's vaccination schedule before the dog is transferred to your care, but your puppy will likely be due for boosters (repeated doses of vaccines that ensure effectiveness) shortly after his homecoming. Bring all the paperwork you received from your breeder to your dog's first appointment so that your veterinarian knows which vaccines have already been administered. Between the rabies vaccine (which cannot be given until a pup is at least 12 weeks old) and boosters for distemper and parvovirus, you will be visiting your veterinarian frequently within the first few months. You will also need to decide if you wish for your Springer to be vaccinated against any optional afflictions, such as kennel cough and Lyme disease.

Bear in mind that while frequent trips to the veterinarian for your dog's initial vaccinations can be both costly and demanding of your time, the best thing you can do for your Springer's health is spread out these inoculations. Some shots already contain several different vaccines. Increasing the number of shots your dog receives in one visit may also increase your Springer's chances of suffering from related

Your English Springer Spaniel will require various vaccinations. Discuss and map out an inoculation routine with your veterinarian.

problems. In mild cases, this may mean side effects such as minor pain, redness, and swelling. In more serious situations, side effects can include anaphylaxis (a severe allergic reaction), autoimmune hemolytic anemia (AIHA), and possibly even death.

Opinions differ somewhat as to the level of these risks, but most veterinarians would agree that limiting the vaccinations your dog receives during a given visit can only help reduce these risks. One Spaniel breeder I know will only administer the distemper combo shot alone. She won't give it with anything else—not the Lyme or rabies vaccine, no heartworm or flea preventative, not even when a dog is in heat.

How Vaccines Work

Commonly made up of infinitesimal amounts of the viruses they aim to prevent, vaccines work by stimulating a dog's own natural immunities. When a vaccine is injected into your Springer's body, it is immediately recognized as a foreign agent. In response, antibodies are rapidly produced to combat this intruder, setting a vital precedent. If the same agent assaults your dog again, its body will respond even more quickly.

Delaying Vaccinations—and Minimizing Costs

If you choose to vaccinate your Springer against several different diseases, be sure to ask your veterinarian about spreading out those shots. Ideally, each inoculation should be administered at least a week or two after the previous one. Many vets only charge a client for an office visit for the first shot, and only for the individual vaccines thereafter. If your vet has no such policy, check with your local pet supply store to see if it holds vaccination clinics for its customers. These common events offer most canine vaccinations—and often additional services, such as microchipping—at a discounted rate. Services are performed by a licensed veterinarian but without the added cost of an exam or office visit. Clinics of this kind should always be used in conjunction with regular veterinary care. Many dog owners ask their vets to administer the first vaccine and then attend clinics

The Vaccination Controversy

Some vaccines are required by law and will need to be given every one to three years. Although laws vary, many cities and counties in the United States have recently lengthened the timetable for the rabies vaccine to three years after reviewing research showing that immunity provided by the vaccine lasts far longer than initially thought. While periodic boosters are necessary, recent findings suggest that vaccinating too frequently may actually be compromising our dogs' immune systems and leaving them particularly vulnerable to other afflictions such as acute allergies, epilepsy, and certain autoimmune diseases.

As with the related issue of how many vaccines are safe to administer at once, members of the veterinary community also have differing views about how often is too often for regular inoculations. The best precaution is to keep abreast of the latest research relating to the safety of all canine vaccinations and making decisions for your dog's care after discussing these issues with a veterinarian you trust. Whatever the problems with the past or current vaccination protocol, abstaining from vaccinating entirely is definitely not the answer. Vaccinations protect your dog from a number of debilitating conditions.

Annual Checkups

Most adult English Springer Spaniels only need to visit their vets once each year. This annual exam provides your vet with an opportunity to check your dog for any physical problems. It also affords you with a chance to get answers to any new questions you may have relating to your dog's care.

In addition to conducting a physical examination, your vet should also draw blood from your Springer each spring to check for certain diseases, such as heartworm and Lyme disease. I schedule my own dogs' exams in the spring annually to cut down on the number of trips we have to make to the vet each year. As a Mainer who detests driving in snowstorms, I am also much less likely to need to reschedule an exam in the spring.

Bringing along a stool sample can help your vet rule out a number of common problems, such as worms. A zip-style plastic bag (remember to turn it inside out before the collection) works great for transport. If you prefer to be discreet, just drop the sealed bag in a small brown paper sack. A sample may be refrigerated for a few hours prior to your appointment, but it should never be frozen.

Scheduling your dog's annual exam for when he needs to be vaccinated is also a smart idea, since it saves you both the hassle and the added expense of an additional office visit. Talk to your vet each year about the vaccines you have opted to give your Springer previously. Perhaps the timetable for booster shots has been lengthened, or maybe your circumstances have changed, making a particular shot less necessary than in the past. If you have moved from a rural area to a suburban community, for example, the possible side effects of the powerful leptospirosis vaccine, a disease predominantly spread through the urine of wildlife, may now outweigh the risks for the disease itself.

Two is a common age for the onset of many physical problems in Springers—including hip dysplasia, progressive retinal atrophy (an eye disease that causes blindness, also known as PRA), and epilepsy. If such a condition strikes your Springer at this age, the good news is that he is still a very young dog, and therefore much more able to cope with such difficulties. In fact, the key to dealing with nearly any canine affliction is early intervention. While many chronic conditions aren't curable, and some typically worsen with age, most are treatable.

As your Springer ages, consider increasing the frequency of his routine veterinary exams. Senior pets should be seen at least twice each year so that any problems can be caught as early as possible. Older pets often have weaker immune systems, making it especially important to nip illnesses in the proverbial bud. Prevention is the most important goal of good veterinary care, but early diagnosis of any problems is a close second.

COMMON HEALTH ISSUES SPRINGERS FACE

Every English Springer Spaniel will face at least a few health problems during his lifetime. While some issues are more common than others, it is important to remember that any dog can be afflicted with any disease or other medical condition at any time. Older Springers are more prone to health problems than are younger ones, but even puppies can face unexpected illnesses. By educating yourself about the most prevalent health problems, you will be able to prevent countless diseases—and diagnose many other problems before they have become serious issues.

Each breed in particular is prone to at least a few maladies. Beware of any breeder who claims otherwise. A good breeder's top priority is to test her dogs for the most common ailments that strike English Springer Spaniels and remove from her breeding program any dogs testing positive for those problems. Unfortunately, owners cannot test for many chronic conditions, such as epilepsy, but breeders should always retire a dog suffering from such a condition as soon as the problem is diagnosed.

Umbilical Hernias

During your Springer puppy's first vet visit, your veterinarian should check his belly button for an umbilical hernia. This is a small rupture in the abdomen. Umbilical hernias may be hereditary, or they may be acquired during the birth process. Most are relatively small—less than 5 millimeters (one-fifth of an inch or less) in diameter—with only a small amount of protruding tissue. Hernias of this size usually pose little risk, but most vets will repair them nonetheless during spaying or neutering if they haven't already closed on their own by this time. Larger umbilical hernias may measure as much as roughly 1 to 2 inches (2 to 6 cm). All large umbilical hernias should be closed, but those in the mid-size range pose particular concern. These can lead to a medical emergency called a strangulated hernia. In this situation, a section of the dog's intestine gets strangulated or trapped within the hernia, cutting off blood supply. Since this is a life-threatening condition, repair should be made as soon as possible.

If your Springer puppy develops a health problem that may be genetic (ask your vet if you are unsure if a problem can be hereditary), be sure to inform your breeder. This will alert the breeder that there may be a problem in the line. A responsible breeder will then inform other people who purchased Springer puppies from that litter so that they can be on the lookout for any signs of the same problem.

Cataracts

Although prevalent, cataracts are fortunately painless and also highly treatable. They may be inherited or caused by a traumatic injury to the dog's eye. The latter type will only affect the eye that has been wounded.

Symptoms

The word "cataract" literally means "to break down"; in the case of this ophthalmologic condition, it is the transparency of the eye's lens that essentially breaks down, leaving an opaque film over the dog's eye. This film (or cataract) that interrupts the dog's vision is usually extremely noticeable to an observant owner.

Treatment

Although there is no way to prevent or reverse cataracts, they can be surgically removed and replaced with an acrylic lens by a veterinary ophthalmologist. This procedure offers an impressive success rate of 90 to 95 percent in otherwise healthy dogs. Interestingly, this statistic remains the same regardless of how long a dog has had cataracts.

A third cause of cataracts can be the onset of diabetes. In this unique situation, the progression of the cataracts may actually be decelerated with successful treatment of the diabetes.

Ear Infections

The English Springer Spaniel's pendulous ears leave the breed particularly vulnerable to ear infections. With the ear leather lying so closely against the ear canal, airflow is severely restricted; this results in trapped moisture—a breeding ground for infection. Although usually caused by bacteria or yeast, ear infections known as otitis externa can also result from wax build-up, an overabundance of hair inside the ear, or a foreign body that has become lodged in the ear canal. They can also be secondary to other kinds of bodily infections. When otitis externa spreads to the middle ear, the result is otitis media, a more serious infection. A ruptured eardrum can also cause otitis media.

Ear Infection Exacerbaters

Factors that may contribute to a Springer's predisposition to ear infections include insufficient drying after bathing or swimming and using too much ear cleanser or harsh products when cleaning the ears. A naturally narrow ear canal can also place a dog at greater risk.

Symptoms

If your Springer is suffering from either type of ear infection, it will be hard to miss the signs. Your dog will likely shake his head or scratch at his ears uncontrollably in response to the discomfort. Tilting of the head in one direction is also a sign of an ear infection. The ear itself may appear red or swollen, with or without a black or yellowish discharge. Often there is also a strong, offensive odor emanating from the infected ear.

At the first sign of an ear infection, bring your dog to a veterinarian for an examination. The vet will need to make sure the eardrum is not ruptured before prescribing a medication, as some drugs can lead to hearing loss if this is the case.

As tempting as it may be to clean the ear before bringing your Springer to be examined, you will be doing both your dog and your vet a favor by abstaining from doing so. Even a mild cleanser will likely irritate your Springer's already sore ear once it is infected, so for now this task is best left for the professionals. Also, being able to look at the ear through an otoscope will help your vet diagnose the problem. She may also wish to take a sample from the ear canal for inspection under a microscope.

Treatment

Once a diagnosis has been made, your vet will probably prescribe an antibiotic to clear up the infection. A middle ear infection can take up to several weeks to resolve completely, but most cases of otitis externa improve relatively quickly once treatment has begun. An ear infection is not a problem that will go away on its own; veterinary treatment must be sought. With proper treatment and sensible precautions taken in the future, however, ear infections don't have to be a recurrent problem.

The conventional Springer haircut, which includes clipping the hair on the face and upper third of the ear short, actually helps prevent ear infections from occurring by maximizing airflow. Trimming the hair inside the ear can also increase air flow.

Your Springer has the long Spaniel ears. They must be cleaned regularly.

Epilepsy

Another condition to which English Springer Spaniels are prone is seizures. Most frequently the result of a condition called idiopathic epilepsy (the word "idiopathic" means that the cause is not known), canine seizures can be frightening for both dogs and owners.

Symptoms

A seizing dog may shake uncontrollably, staring into space (typically signs of a petit mal seizure) or fall to his side, drool, and make a paddling motion with his legs (signs of a grand mal seizure)—all for no apparent reason. Sometimes prior to or after a seizure, the dog may pant heavily and lose control of his bladder or bowels.

The most important thing to remember if your dog ever experiences a seizure is probably one of the most difficult: remain calm.

Treatment

There are many old wives' tales about seizures, including the notion that an animal can swallow his tongue during the episode; rest assured this is not the case. Putting your fingers in the mouth of a seizing animal can, however, be dangerous for you, as even the most amiable dog may bite when in the midst of the experience. Making sure your dog does not harm himself (by bumping into anything, for instance) is a good idea, but keep your hands and face away from your dog's mouth at all times.

The most important thing to remember if your dog ever experiences a seizure is probably one of the most difficult—and that is to remain calm. Doing so will help you best observe what is happening so that you can relay this information to your

When Two Minutes Feels Like a Lifetime

When I first began writing books about dogs, I thankfully had very little first-hand experience with epilepsy. I'd had friends and family members with epileptic dogs, but I had never witnessed a canine seizure personally. In 2005, however, one of my own dogs suffered her first seizure and was diagnosed with the disease shortly thereafter. Although we manage her illness with medication, Molly still has a seizure every three or four months. Our veterinarian has explained that the goal is not to prevent the seizures entirely—this simply isn't possible—but to limit their frequency, length, and intensity as much as we can.

Watching Molly seize is one of the most difficult things I have ever experienced. In the beginning, I became a total wreck whenever this happened. Tears would stream down my face, and I think I shook nearly as much as she did. Each episode seemed to last forever, even though in reality most of them were less than two minutes long. Over time, however, I realized that my falling apart did nothing to help Molly, and her well-being is my first priority. If anything positive has come from her ongoing seizures, it is that through them I have learned more about how to best help Molly both during and after an episode. I have even gotten fairly good at predicting them by watching both the calendar and her behavior.

Even my eight-year-old son now knows the protocol: *As soon as you notice a seizure starting, sit down on the floor and hold her gently. Stroke her head softly, while speaking to her in a calm voice. Stay away from her face, but remain close, so she knows she's not alone. Watch the clock to get an accurate time reading, and call the vet as soon as it's over, so the seizure can be recorded in her chart.*

If your Springer suffers from epilepsy, I highly recommend a book titled *Canine Epilepsy: An Owner's Guide to Living With and Without Seizures* by Caroline D. Levin, R.N. I have found this to be an invaluable resource for understanding and dealing with Molly's chronic condition. Levin has also written an equally helpful book about canine blindness called *Living With Blind Dogs: A Resource Book and Training Guide for the Owners of Blind and Low-Vision Dogs.* Both titles are available through book retailers nationwide.

veterinarian. If the seizure passes within a few minutes, you can wait to contact your vet until it has passed. If it continues longer than this, however, you should bring your dog to the veterinary hospital immediately. Because seizures can sometimes be a sign of other illnesses, such as liver disease, kidney disease, and cancer, your dog should be examined to help rule out these conditions. Your vet may suggest running a blood profile for this reason. Idiopathic epilepsy is usually the reason for seizures in dogs less than five years of age, but older dogs are at a higher risk of problems that might be the culprit, such as a tumor in the central nervous system.

If your Springer has suffered one or more idiopathic seizures, you may wish to start keeping a journal of the incidences.

Record the date and time, the length of the seizure, a detailed description of what happens during the episode, and also a brief account of what happens before and after the seizure. This information could be especially helpful to your vet in regards to your dog's treatment plan.

Fortunately, idiopathic epilepsy is usually highly manageable. Despite the frightening nature of the disease, the long-term prognosis for most cases is usually quite good. In many situations, treatment isn't even necessary. If your dog is experiencing seizures more often than once a month, or if the episodes are lasting several minutes each, your vet may suggest placing your dog on an oral anticonvulsant medication. The most common of these is phenobarbital.

Food Allergies

It is estimated that 20 percent of dogs in the United States suffer from some type of allergy. While many veterinarians insist that the risk of food allergies is consistent among all dog breeds, some clinical findings suggest that English Springer Spaniels (along with several other breeds) are indeed predisposed to this problem. My first Spaniel, Jonathan, suffered from two different food allergies. He was allergic to both tomatoes and potatoes.

Because food allergies can develop over time, your dog may suddenly experience an adverse reaction to a food or ingredient that has never been an issue in the past. (When Jonathan was a puppy, I invariably gave him my last potato chip whenever I indulged in the salty treat, and at that time he showed no intolerance to the snack whatsoever.) This kind of unprecedented reaction can make identifying the cause of your dog's allergy difficult but not impossible.

Symptoms

The most common symptom of a canine food allergy is severe itching. A dog may react by incessantly scratching, biting, licking, or rubbing the itchy area—often to the point of inflicting self-trauma. Although rare, a dog may also show gastrointestinal signs of an allergy to a particular food. My Johnny would inevitably vomit every time a guest would unknowingly aggravate the situation by sharing a potato chip or small piece of pizza with him. (At one point, I actually considered hanging a sign in my kitchen reading Please Don't Feed the Dog!) Other dogs may suffer from diarrhea as an effect of the offending food. In some instances, there may be a discharge from the eyes or nose; an affected dog may even cough or sneeze. Seizures and asthmatic reactions have been reported as symptoms of severe canine food allergies.

Your Springer may have an allergic reaction to certain foods. A wide variety of foods and diets are available for you to offer your pet, so if one causes such a reaction, there are others available that you can try.

Treatment

If you or your vet suspects that your Springer is suffering from a food allergy, placing your dog on a hypoallergenic diet can help determine the cause (or causes) of the reaction. These specialized (or prescription) diets are frequently available only through veterinarians. Common canine food allergens include corn, beef, dairy products, wheat, and soybeans. Although allergy tests are available, they can be relatively expensive and not always accurate. Once your dog has demonstrated a tolerance for the specialized diet (usually after at least several weeks), new ingredients may be added back into your dog's feeding regimen one at a time so that you can tell which foods are the likeliest causes of the allergic reactions. Owners must be patient through this challenging process, which can take up to several months.

Don't let an apparent allergy go untreated. Dogs do not understand that persistent scratching can cause secondary issues, such as

infections; they will simply react to itching by
scratching in one form or another every time.
Medicated shampoos and conditioners and
topical creams, ointments, or sprays may
offer some relief, but whenever possible,
avoiding the allergen altogether is best.
Bringing your dog to the vet at the first sign
of an allergy can place your dog on the
road to identification before a serious
secondary problem is triggered.

Hip or Elbow Dysplasia

When many of us hear the term "hip dysplasia,"
we immediately think of larger breeds such as
German Shepherds and Labrador Retrievers, but
surprisingly this problem is also quite common in
smaller breeds like the English Springer Spaniel.
Although good breeders test for hip dysplasia, it
can still occasionally appear in some dogs that
have been cleared; there is no way to guarantee that
a dog won't develop the condition. Literally a malformation of
the ball and socket in the hip joint, hip dysplasia is an inherited
defect that usually doesn't develop until a dog is between six to
eight months old.

Symptoms

Although the condition may be mild, moderate, or severe, the
signs are usually the same, including lameness, stiffness, and
limping. Symptoms may be intensified on cold, damp days. A
dog suffering from hip dysplasia may also exhibit an
understandable change in temperament.

As the dog continues, however reluctantly, to move through
the pain, the problem may seem to dissipate, but more likely
this is simply the result of scar tissue that forms from the
stretching and tearing of the joint. Eventually, arthritis also sets
in and compounds the problem when symptoms return.

Treatment

Diagnosis is made through veterinary examination and x-
rays. A veterinarian may recommend surgery in extreme cases,

but medical treatment is also possible. This may include enforced rest periods during times of acute discomfort, mild analgesics (pain killers), and anti-inflammatory drugs. Although surgical treatment may seem like a risky endeavor, many dogs return to a full activity level even after having a full hip replacement.

Hypothyroidism (Low Thyroid)

Like people, dogs have two small, butterfly-shaped lobes situated at the back of their necks called the thyroid gland. While this gland is responsible for a number of functions within the body, its primary task is controlling your Springer's metabolism, the rate at which your dog processes his daily caloric intake from food. Hypothyroidism is a condition in which the thyroid gland becomes underactive, therefore leaving the affected dog particularly vulnerable to weight gain, loss of energy, and many other unpleasant side effects. A dog suffering from hypothyroidism may also experience skin problems, chronic ear infections, and even depression.

Symptoms

Weight gain is often the most blatant symptom of this condition, so inform your veterinarian if your Springer's weight has suddenly increased without an apparent explanation, such as a more voracious appetite.

Treatment

If your vet suspects hypothyroidism, one or more blood tests will be used to confirm the diagnosis. It is important to note that a number of different testing methods are available for diagnosing this condition, each with its own level of accuracy. Usually more than one type of test is necessary for a reliable diagnosis. Although the differences between the tests may seem complex, your vet can explain the basic principles of each so that you can make an informed decision.

Once diagnosed, hypothyroidism may be treated with a daily dose of a synthetic thyroid hormone called thyroxine (levothyroxine). Although periodic checkups will be necessary to ensure proper dosing, most dogs with hypothyroidism remain symptom-free for the rest of their lives.

Aggression and Thyroid

Various illnesses can make a dog act aggressively, but many vets have noticed a specific link between aggression and abnormally low thyroid levels. If your dog suddenly starts acting aggressively at an older age, schedule an appointment with his vet and ask her to check his thyroid.

Progressive Retinal Atrophy (PRA)

Progressive retinal atrophy (PRA) is an inherited degenerative disorder that causes gradual but inevitable vision loss.

Symptoms

A Springer with PRA will likely begin bumping into things only at night or in low-light situations, but will eventually show signs of increasing vision loss regardless of the time of day or quality of light. Although PRA has further symptoms (including dilated pupils and hyperreflectivity, or shininess, to the back of the eye), these signs are rarely noticeable until the disease has already reached an advanced stage.

Treatment

Having your Springer tested for the mutated gene that causes PRA is both simple and fairly inexpensive. A blood test is all that is needed; it may take a few weeks to get the results. Even if your dog tests affected for the disease, however, there is no way to know for certain when (or even if) he will begin losing his eyesight. For some owners, knowing where the risk factors lie can help them prepare for dealing with this situation down the road. If you would like to have your Springer tested for the PRA gene, ask your vet about this new test.

Springers with progressive retinal atrophy can live a long and happy life.

If every cloud indeed has a silver lining—for PRA, it is the amount of time that an owner is given to help prepare for her dog's eventual sight loss—even if the dog was never tested for the PRA gene. As the name of the disease implies, vision loss progresses slowly. Although it is natural for an owner to feel overwhelmed at first by the prognosis of permanent blindness, it is important to realize that your English Springer Spaniel will be impacted by this deficit far less than a human in a similar situation. Blind dogs can live enormously satisfying lives. Although some additional training

will be necessary, most sightless Springers acclimate to this change easily by simply doing what they have always done—relying on their other, more valued senses, particularly hearing and smell.

If your dog has PRA, give yourself some time to accept this unpleasant turn of events, but know that the ordeal won't be nearly as dreadful as you might fear. After an initial adjustment period, both you and your dog will be able to enjoy a surprisingly normal life together despite your Springer's visual impairment.

Skin Problems

Although some skin problems are secondary to other issues (such as food allergies), English Springer Spaniels have a predisposition to a skin condition called primary seborrhea, caused by an overproduction of skin cells, including sebaceous (oil) cells.

Symptoms

Dogs suffering from primary seborrhea may have greasy and

scaly skin. A foul odor may also be present. Eventually lesions form, most commonly on the elbows, hocks, and ears. The skin may or may not itch.

Treatment

Primary seborrhea is considered a chronic condition. Although there is no cure, treatment with medicated shampoos, ointments, antibiotics, or corticosteroids can be helpful in managing the condition.

OTHER COMMON CANINE HEALTH PROBLEMS

Arthritis

As your English Springer Spaniel gets older, he may develop soreness in his joints called arthritis.

Symptoms

The most noticeable sign of arthritis is painful movement. A dog suffering from arthritis may have a hard time standing up, climbing stairs, or walking for long periods of time. Pain is typically worse in the morning, but rain or cold weather can also exacerbate the problem.

Treatment

If you suspect that your Springer has arthritis, schedule an exam with your veterinarian. Once the problem has been diagnosed, your vet can help you create a plan of action to ease your dog's pain. There is no cure for arthritis, but the condition can be managed. Pain medications can offer patients relief. Many owners have also witnessed marked improvement after giving their dogs dietary supplements containing glucosamine, chondroitin, and methylsulfonylmethane (MSM). Talk you to your vet about the best combinations and doses for your Springer based on his weight and age.

Making changes to your dog's environment can also ease the pain of arthritis. If your dog sleeps in a crate, make sure it is positioned away from any drafts from doors or windows. Also, check the liner. Over time a padded liner can go from thick and luxurious to thin and threadbare. The orthopedic foam that is so popular for mattresses made for people is also available in many pet products. It is an excellent material for both crate liners and dog beds.

If your Springer sleeps with you at night, jumping on and off your bed may be aggravating his pain. Special steps made specifically for dogs to access furniture more easily are now available in many pet supply stores. It may take you a short time to teach your dog to use his staircase faithfully, but it can be done. And many owners prefer training their dogs to use the steps, rather than crating their pets for the first time as seniors.

Anything that makes your Springer more comfortable can help make the arthritis take less of a toll. Even if your dog sleeps with you, consider placing a dog bed somewhere else in your home where he spends a great deal of time. Even an arthritic dog may enjoy sleeping on a tile floor, since it can feel good on their bellies, but doing so can be bad for his joints. A safety gate can help you block your dog's access to areas where he shouldn't be spending large amounts of time.

Cancer

At one time cancer was a diagnosis that offered little hope— to either people or pets. Thankfully, however, more and more human and canine patients who face this menacing illness are beating it. Smart owners keep a close eye on their pets for signs that something isn't right. And the most important step in fighting almost any type of cancer is early diagnosis.

Symptoms

When grooming or cuddling with your Springer, check his body for any lumps or bumps that may have appeared. If you find one, contact your veterinarian. She may suggest taking a biopsy. If so, try not to panic. Many growths turn out to be benign fatty tumors. Many Springers develop these with age. Unless they interfere with your dog's comfort and mobility, in fact, they do not even have to be removed. If a growth turns out to be malignant, don't despair. You have already stacked the odds in your dog's favor by finding it early.

An external tumor is in one way a blessing—owners are able to see it and consequently take action quickly. Internal tumors can be a bit more insidious. Symptoms of an internal malignancy include swelling, bleeding or discharge from any body cavity, difficulty breathing, and persistent coughing. Other signs can be more vague—a decreased appetite, for example. Listen to your instincts, and remember—you know your dog best. If you suspect something is wrong, don't be afraid to schedule a vet appointment even if your dog exhibits no tangible signs of illness. An extra exam won't harm your pet, but identifying an illness like cancer as early as possible can save his life.

Treatment

Treatment options for cancer include surgery, radiation or chemotherapy, and even holistic treatments like acupuncture. Nutritional changes can also play an important role. Which course of action is best for your dog depends on his individual circumstances.

Obesity

One of the most common issues adult dogs face is obesity. Just like most people, a dog's metabolism slows with age. Even if your Springer is eating the same amount of food and getting the same amount of exercise as he did as a younger dog, this means he may still start to pack on some unwanted pounds.

Regular exercise—no matter the season—will keep your Springer happy and healthy.

Symptoms

A fit English Springer Spaniel should weigh between 40 and 50 pounds (18 and 23 kg). Males typically fall at the heavier end of this spectrum, with females on the lighter side. To make sure your dog hasn't gained too much weight, step on your bathroom scale with him from time to time, deducting your own weight from what the two of you weigh together. A great way to do a quick check for obesity is by feeling your dog's ribs. They should be discernible but not prominent. If you have to press deeply into your dog's body to feel his ribs, chances are your Springer is overweight.

Treatment

Your vet may suggest cutting back on your dog's kibble or switching to a weight-loss formula, as well as increasing your dog's exercise. If your Springer is truly obese, you may need to work on the former part of the plan for a while before increasing his activity level. Helping your dog lose weight will be a time-consuming process, but it will be worth your effort. Being overweight increases your dog's risks for a number of diseases—including arthritis and diabetes. By keeping your Springer within an acceptable weight range, you will help him live a longer, more comfortable life.

DEALING WITH PARASITES

For many English Springer Spaniel owners, just thinking about fleas and ticks is enough to prompt scratching. Our pets, though, have to deal with a bit more than itchy discomfort when confronted by these dangerous pests. The creatures have an uncanny knack for seeking out our precious pets and exposing them to a number of serious diseases. Fortunately, these illnesses can easily be avoided by using simple preventive medications sold at most veterinary hospitals and also by a variety of new pet pharmacies that offer impressively competitive prices.

You will need to visit your dog's veterinarian before ordering preventive medication from a pet pharmacy, as a prescription is necessary. Generally, though, this process is a simple one. Many companies will even contact your vet on your behalf before dispensing the medications.

Fleas

To some owners, fleas may seem like a fact of canine life—one that, in comparison to other parasitic pests, is more an annoyance than a danger. But the fact is that these bothersome creatures can cause serious illness. Most dogs are allergic to the flea saliva left behind on their skin after the biting begins, and many will react automatically by scratching to the point of creating sores and skin infection. If left untreated, flea infestation can lead to anemia and even the transmission of tapeworms. For puppies and elderly pets, these effects can be disastrous, even deadly.

Although wingless, fleas are capable of jumping distances of 13 inches (33 cm) or farther horizontally, making it possible for them to spread from one animal to another with great efficiency. They also reproduce at an astounding rate, leaving entire households vulnerable to the havoc they wreak.

Signs

Fleas can be difficult to locate on dogs with much shorter coats; on a Springer they can be virtually impossible to pinpoint, but persistent scratching is usually a reliable indicator of their presence. They usually target specific areas on a dog, including near the ears, on the neck and abdomen, and around the base of the tail.

Prevention and Treatment

The problem of fleas can easily be prevented, but the method of prevention you choose can drastically affect both the outcome and your dog's health. The safest and most effective route for combating fleas is using preventive treatments recommended by your veterinarian. Some brands even prevent fleas and ticks with just a single medication. The majority of preventive treatments are applied topically to a small section of your dog's skin once a month. Once applied, the solution is absorbed through the skin and spreads, eliminating any fleas presently hiding within your dog's coat and preventing future infestation.

If your Springer has fleas, you will need to take several important steps to eliminate the problem for good. First, see your veterinarian at once. In addition to treating your dog, you will also need to treat your dog's environment, which may span

See your veterinarian if you think your Springer has fleas.

from the inside of your home to your backyard. Your vet's input can be invaluable in selecting the best plan of attack.

Because fleas thrive in warm temperatures, your home is an ideal haven for these long-lasting pests—even in the middle of winter. Carpets, furniture, and draperies all provide excellent refuge. Your house may be the cleanest on the block, and it won't make a bit of difference; the fleas will still make themselves right at home. They will also feast on any available target—your dog, your cat, even your children and you.

The most effective flea bombs (or foggers) are highly toxic, so it is imperative that you read and follow all instructions very carefully. It is particularly important that you remove all people and pets from your home before treating it. If your home contains carpeting, remember to vacuum thoroughly after treatment is completed, and don't forget to throw away the bag immediately whether it is full or not. It only takes a single flea to start a second wave of infestation.

Be sure to check with your veterinarian before using any over-the-counter flea or tick product. Organophosphate insecticides (OPs) and carbamates are found in various products and should be avoided, since they pose particular health threats to children and pets even when used correctly. A product contains an OP if the ingredient list contains chlorpyrifos, dichlorvos, phosmet, naled, tetrachlorvinphos, diazinon, or malathion. The product contains a carbamate if the ingredient list includes carbaryl or propoxur.

Natural products that are gentler for treating both pets and their environments are available. For example, herbal flea collars, sprays, and shampoos can be purchased as an alternative to those containing pesticides. These products will repel fleas rather than kill them, so it is important to also use flea-trapping devices when going this route. Natural products sometimes also contain ingredients known for strengthening the canine immune system, since unhealthy dogs are especially prone to fleas and other parasites.

Heartworm

Heartworm, perhaps the best known of all canine parasites, is passed from dog to dog by way of mosquito bites. Even if you live in a colder climate, your dog is still at risk for this deadly disease. Since mosquitoes can exist in temperatures as low as 57°F (14°C), this means there are virtually no safe havens. Heartworm has been reported in dogs from all 50 states. As an added safety precaution, some veterinarians now even recommend the use of monthly (or daily) preventatives year round. When used correctly, these protective treatments are approximately 100 percent effective. As an added advantage, heartworm preventive eliminates other intestinal parasites that may be in your dog's system, such as hookworms and roundworms.

Signs

Because dogs recently or lightly infected with heartworms may show no signs of the disease, it is important to have your dog's blood tested annually, preferably in the spring. Even if your dog is on a year-round preventive regimen, your Springer may become infected after just a single missed dose. Once a dog begins to show symptoms, they are likely to be severe, including coughing, exercise intolerance, and respiratory distress.

As the name implies, this disease targets a dog's heart, but the initial damage actually occurs in the lungs, where the heartworm infiltrates the animal's blood vessels, causing them to swell and become scarred. As blood flow becomes more and more restricted, blood pressure rises, resulting in hypertension. Without intervention, heart failure eventually ensues.

Prevention and Treatment

If your dog is diagnosed with heartworm disease, the prognosis will depend on how far the disease has progressed and whether there are any secondary conditions, such as liver or kidney problems. At one time, treatment itself was a dangerous undertaking, but new medications have made treating even dogs with severe infestations considerably safer. Still, prevention is highly preferred. Although treatment is now indeed less dangerous, it remains a complicated and expensive procedure.

Ticks

Ticks can carry some of the most menacing diseases in existence today. One of the best ways to tell a tick from less harmful insects is by counting its legs. Being an arachnid, a tick will have eight of them, while an insect will only have six. Unlike most insects, ticks will also attach themselves to their hosts with great force, often making removal difficult.

Signs

Many ticks are extremely small and can therefore be extremely difficult to see in their normal state. For example, an

Look for Ticks

Ticks can spread a number of canine diseases — including Lyme disease, Rocky Mountain spotted fever, and tick paralysis.

adult deer tick (which spreads Lyme disease) is about 2.5 millimeters (one-tenth of an inch)—about the size of a sesame seed. Once ticks attach themselves to their chosen hosts, however, they begin engorging on the hosts' blood. An adult Rocky Mountain wood tick typically falls between 2.1 and 6.1 millimeters (less than one-tenth to one-fifth of an inch) in length, but can measure as much as 16.5 millimeters (about three-fifths of an inch) when engorged. The longer a tick is attached to your dog, the more engorged it will get, but you want to find and remove any tick that attacks your pet as soon as possible to avoid infection. If you take your dog for frequent walks in the woods, doing a tick check should become a standard part of your routine. It is important to note, however, that ticks are not restricted to the woods and high grass. They can also frequent suburban backyards or public parks.

Prevention and Treatment

Check your Springer regularly for ticks if he spends a lot of time outdoors.

The same monthly treatment you use to prevent fleas from accosting your English Springer Spaniel should also prevent ticks from attaching themselves to your pet. Because owners can

How to Remove a Tick

If you find a tick on your dog, use a pair of tweezers to carefully remove it. Since it is vital that you get both the tick's head and body out, your first objective will be getting the tick to simply let go on its own. To do this, use a pair of sterilized tweezers to grasp the tick's body and begin pulling it away from your dog's skin very gently. Apply steady pressure, but be sure not to squeeze too tightly. Jiggling the tick a bit is fine, but don't rotate it.

Some vets suggest using a drop or two of isopropyl alcohol to get a tick to release a stubborn grip, but according to the American Lyme Disease Foundation, this method can backfire, even increasing the chances of disease transmission. Once the tick is out, this is the time for the alcohol—drop the tick in some of this solution to kill it. Never use your bare hands or feet to kill a tick. As soon as the tick has been properly disposed of, clean the bite wound with disinfectant, and sterilize your tweezers with some fresh alcohol.

If you cannot get the tick to release, or if you remove only part of it, seek assistance from your veterinarian.

sometimes forget to administer this medication on time, however, it is still a wise idea to check your dog regularly, especially if you live in a high-risk area of the country, such as New England where I live.

Worms

Some dogs also face another unpleasant parasite commonly called worms. These relentless organisms grow, feed, and take shelter within your dog's gastrointestinal system; in fact 34 percent of dogs in the United States harbor such a parasite.

Signs

Checking your dog's stool regularly may help identify the presence of some types of worms (roundworms and tapeworms, for example), but others (such as whipworms and hookworms) can be much less conspicuous. Signs indicating worms include excessive licking of the anal region or a persistent dragging of the rear end.

Prevention and Treatment

Because worms are parasites capable of spreading to human family members, an ounce of prevention may be worth even more than the proverbial pound of cure. Keeping your yard free of your dog's feces is an excellent way to lower your dog's risk of suffering from most kinds of worms. The soil contamination caused by this excrement provides ideal conditions for many of these worms. It is also a wise idea to bring along a stool sample every time you visit the vet. What isn't visible to your naked eye will likely be much clearer under a microscope.

If your dog is diagnosed with worms, follow the instructions of your veterinarian carefully. Most importantly, never give your dog a wormer (a common name for the medication intended to rid a dog's body of worms) without your vet's knowledge and approval. If treatment is recommended, however, don't forget to ask your vet about treating your dog's environment as well, to prevent further infestation.

COMPLEMENTARY MEDICINE

Complementary medicine is an umbrella term for a number of ancient healing techniques that have been used in the Far East for thousands of years. At one time, many Westerners referred to complementary therapies as "alternative medicine,"

You may want to explore alternative veterinary therapies for your Springer.

since they viewed these modalities as separate from conventional medicine. You may have heard the word "holistic" used to describe complementary therapies, as well. This is because so many forms of complementary medicine involve treating the whole person, not simply a disease or injury. The word "holistic" means whole.

Like many other people, I used to think of holistic treatments as the strategies one might consider only when conventional methods failed. I never really looked down on complementary methods—I even had first-hand experience with successful chiropractic treatment for migraines, but still, whenever I had a problem, I always sought standard medical treatment first. It took a holistic experience with my dog, however, to show me that complementary methods can be a wonderful first choice for health care.

Acupuncture

An ancient form of Chinese medicine, acupuncture can be traced back at least 2,500 years. By inserting tiny needles into specific points on the body, an acupuncturist aims to release healing energy within the body, called *qi* (pronounced CHEE). While many people have a hard time getting beyond the mechanics of this modality, proponents of acupuncture insist that, much like human patients, animals feel absolutely no pain from the threadlike needles.

The American Veterinary Medical Association (AVMA) acknowledges acupuncture as "an integral part of veterinary medicine." This is no small endorsement. Perhaps better than anything else, the AVMA's approval shows pet owners that complementary techniques are not as off-the-wall as they may initially seem. Whether used alone or in conjunction with conventional methods, complementary modalities can offer impressive success. To find a canine acupuncturist in your area, contact the American Academy of Veterinary Acupuncture (AAVA) at www.aava.org.

My Exprience With Acupuncture

My son was just an infant the winter my dog Jonathan fell on the ice in our backyard one night. The diagnosis wasn't good: a ruptured anterior cruciate ligament. To make matters even worse, he had torn the meniscus (a type of cartilage) within his knee. This all made it extremely painful for him to bear any weight on his back leg. The veterinarian at the emergency clinic told me that surgery would be unavoidable—and that it would involve a three-month recovery period, during which I would have to carry Johnny virtually everywhere. I scheduled a follow-up appointment with my regular vet as I tried to imagine how I would manage getting my dog outdoors to relieve himself several times each day with an eight-month-old baby in tow. Still, I was determined to do whatever was necessary to help my injured dog.

When I brought Jonathan to my vet, my anxiety over the situation was obvious. Just the word "surgery" set me on edge. One of the factors that likely led to Johnny's fall was his increased weight, which also posed risks for him in undergoing anesthesia. Was there any other option?

My vet then asked if I would consider having her perform some acupuncture before going the surgical route. She told me that she'd had impressive success in the past in using acupuncture to treat this type of injury and that avoiding surgery could significantly reduce the amount of scar tissue that ultimately developed. This would translate to a reduced chance of arthritis down the road. She couldn't guarantee a positive outcome (heck, not even the operation could do that), but she wanted to know if I thought it was worth trying. I was practically searching her exam room cupboards for the needles before she was done asking the question.

I scheduled Jonathan's first acupuncture session that day at my vet's office and started him on a supplement containing glucosamine when we returned home to stimulate the growth of new cartilage in his knee. My vet had shown me the needles she would be using, I suspect to ease my anxiety a bit more. It worked. The needles, which I had imagined as looking like spikes, instead resembled thin hairs. Without the holders on the ends, I might have even had a difficult time seeing them.

At our first appointment, the vet began by placing a single needle at the back of Jonathan's head. Placing a needle at this acupuncture point, she explained, would help calm him. He wasn't a rambunctious dog by any means, but I did wonder how she was going to get him to sit still while she inserted the rest of the needles, some very close to the still tender spot of his injury. Within minutes, Johnny was lying on his side, as if he had suddenly become rather drowsy. I am told that some dogs actually fall asleep during treatment, although Jonathan never did.

Next, the vet inserted the remaining needles—about a dozen in all—one at a time at various spots down Johnny's back and bad leg. She then heated each needle with an item that looked like a lit cigar. It was actually a type of incense that was also intended to stimulate relaxation. The heat from the incense, she said, triggered healing in the area of each needle it touched. Some vets use a small battery-charged device to provide electrical stimulation for a similar purpose.

We began with three treatments a week, an undeniably hectic schedule. As Johnny's leg seemed to improve, though, we then dropped our appointments progressively—first to twice a week, then to once, and then once every other week. The entire process took about three months, the same amount of time the recovery from that dreaded surgery would have taken. It also cost about the same amount. But my vet managed to bring Johnny's leg back to normal functioning without ever having to anesthetize him or operate. We also managed to get Jonathan's weight down to a reasonable number, so anesthesia wouldn't pose such a risk if he ever did need surgery in the future.

Chiropractic Care

Chiropractic care is another form of medicine that often draws the disdain of skeptics, but like other forms of complementary medicine, it often provides legitimate relief from many canine health problems. Focusing on the spine and joints, a veterinary chiropractor does not diagnose disease, but rather treats symptoms directly. Chiropractic care literally addresses vertebral subluxations—dislocations of the bones or joints surrounding the spinal column that may be hindering the animal's health.

Like the AAVA for acupuncture, the American Veterinary Chiropractic Association (AVCA) can direct you to a qualified veterinary chiropractor in your area. Visit the AVCA on the web at www.animalchiropractic.org. A chiropractor may be able to help if your dog suffers from lameness, seizures, or other chronic health problems. Your conventional veterinarian may also refer you to a chiropractor if your dog experiences an injury requiring this kind of expertise.

A Note on Complementary Therapy

Remember that complementary therapies, like conventional medicine, are not an exact science. There is no way to know for certain which method will best serve your Springer's needs. Sometimes results take time, but if something doesn't feel right, perhaps this particular method isn't the best one for your dog's problem. The very basis of the holistic approach is treating the whole being. Beware of any caregiver who doesn't take the time and effort to evaluate your dog completely. These few undesirable individuals can give the world of complementary medicine a bad name. However, when used correctly, this diverse resource can offer your pet many worthwhile options for improved health and well-being.

Homeopathy

Like acupuncture, homeopathy stimulates the body to heal itself. Based on a very similar principle as the vaccination process, homeopathic medicine works by implementing infinitesimal doses of the substances that actually cause the disease a caregiver wishes to cure. While the amounts of the substances used in homeopathy are far removed from that of a vaccination, the premise of homeopathy is that the more these substances are diluted, the more powerful the effect on the patient will be.

When treated with homeopathic medicine, a dog may actually exhibit an intensification of symptoms before improvement begins. A Springer with a fever, for example, may at first experience an even higher temperature. The ultimate goal, however, is a complete removal of all symptoms by creating a natural resistance to the illness.

Homeopathy is not something in which dog owners should dabble. Although it may be tempting to apply any knowledge you may already have in this area to your dog's current condition, it is always best to seek the advice of a trained professional, preferably a licensed veterinarian who is also trained in this particular branch of complementary medicine. Since the process involves such precise dosages, a high level of vigilance in treatment is mandatory.

Physical Therapy

The field of physical therapy is one of the most expanding professions within the human medical care community. People rely on this productive resource for help with all kinds of physical issues ranging from hip dysplasia to strokes. It makes sense that canine patients suffering from these same problems can benefit from the canine version of this effective treatment.

You can ask your veterinarian for recommendations for alternative veterinary therapies.

With the aid of such technological tools as ultrasound and electrical stimulation, canine physical therapists often start where conventional veterinarians leave off—after surgical procedures, during the healing of an injury to increase range of motion and overall strength, and even as a means of reducing pain and stiffness associated with a variety of chronic conditions. Canine physical therapists also utilize more traditional modalities such as massage, hydrotherapy, and therapeutic exercise. The exact combination of treatments depends on your dog's individual needs.

Any veterinarian can legally perform canine physical therapy, but it is important to note that very few vets receive training in this area as part of their formal education. Ideally, I recommend looking for a veterinarian who is also a licensed physical therapist for human patients. If you have trouble finding one of these dually trained individuals, however, expand your search to find both a veterinarian and physical therapist who are willing to work together for the betterment of your English Springer Spaniel's health.

Canine Massage

Canine massage, although a component of many different complementary approaches, is a wondrous technique in its own right. On a more basic level, dog owners can even perform it at home for the mere pleasure it provides their pets. With just a small amount of instruction, you can simultaneously ease any tension your dog may be feeling and also offer your canine companion several health benefits, including increased circulation, relaxation of muscle spasms, and even lowered blood pressure. Think of how good a back rub feels to us; of course our dogs enjoy this simple indulgence, too.

Never perform canine massage or any other kind of complementary medicine without proper instruction from a qualified provider. Also, remember that no procedure should ever be used as a substitute for licensed veterinary care. Many good books and videos are available about the use of canine massage in the home. Your dog's individual reaction is paramount; listen to it, and let it be your guide. You may be doing everything by the book, but if your dog shows any signs of displeasure, stop the massage immediately. Most dogs enjoy being massaged, but just like people, our dogs have a way of letting us know when something isn't right for them.

EMERGENCY FIRST AID

If your English Springer Spaniel is involved in a medical emergency, the most important thing for you to do is remain calm. Not only can rash actions spurred by anxiety make your dog's situation even worse, but animals also possess an uncanny ability to sense a human's nervousness. You can unintentionally scare your Springer if you don't pay attention to your own verbal and physical reactions. Bring your dog to the closest veterinarian immediately, calling to let the hospital know you are on your way if possible. Also, depending on the type of emergency, there may be things you can do to help ensure a positive outcome.

A dog's body is very different from a person's in many ways. For this reason, canine first aid differs dramatically from our human perceptions of emergency care. Medical doctors are taught very early in their careers that the first rule of medicine is to do no harm. This is also excellent advice for all

dog owners. Never give your dog any medication without first checking with your veterinarian. Drugs that can help people, such as acetaminophen and ibuprofen, can be fatal for animals. Also, procedures such as the Heimlich maneuver, need to be performed very differently on a choking Springer than on a 200-pound (90-kg) man.

Canine CPR

Cardio-pulmonary resuscitation (CPR) is a combination of rescue breathing and chest compressions delivered to victims of cardiac arrest. This technique, which is regularly used on humans, can also be used on animals in similar emergency situations. The worst time to learn canine CPR, however, is during an emergency. You can ask your veterinarian if any organizations in your area offer courses in canine CPR, or check out the valuable resources available from the Humane Society of the United States (HSUS) and the American Red Cross. If your Springer is not breathing and you don't know how to perform canine CPR, bring the dog to a veterinarian at once.

Choking

Choking may have a number of possible causes, including any small object that can get lodged in your Springer's trachea. Choking is a veterinary emergency, and immediate assistance is necessary. A dog who is choking may drool, gag, struggle to breathe, paw at his face, and regurgitate.

If you think your Springer is choking, first remove his collar (if present), and then examine the inside of the dog's mouth. It is very important that you do not simply pull on any object you may feel in your dog's throat, as dogs have small bones that support the base of their tongues that can easily be mistaken for the object in question. If you cannot identify or remove the object, lift your dog up with his head pointing downwards. This might dislodge the object.

If this doesn't work, you will need to perform a modified Heimlich maneuver. Holding the dog around his waist so that his bottom is closest to you, place a fist just behind the ribs. Compress the abdomen several times (begin with three) with quick upward pressure, and again check the mouth. Even if you are able to dislodge the object and your dog appears fine, it is a good idea to see your veterinarian immediately in case of any internal injury.

Cuts

Lacerations to paws and pads are among the most common canine injuries. Applying firm pressure over a wet gauze pad should stop minor bleeding. Silver nitrate sticks are also useful for speeding the clotting process. To prevent debris from contaminating the wound, flush it with wound cleaning solution, saline solution, or plain water before covering. Once the bleeding has stopped and the laceration has been cleaned,

Cuts and scratches need to be treated immediately to prevent infection.

cover the wound with a nonstick pad and secure it with a bandage.

If your Springer experiences a serious cut, apply a gauze pad soaked in cold water to the wound, and then contact your veterinarian. Do not use absorbent cotton, as it can adhere to the cut and leave fibers in the wound. If blood is spurting from the wound, the dog has most likely severed an artery and needs to be taken to a veterinary hospital immediately.

Dehydration and Heatstroke

Dehydration and heatstroke are usually highly preventable problems. Although your Springer may love the sun, pay attention to your local weather report and any warnings of especially dangerous times to be outdoors. Since dogs only have sweat glands on the pads of their feet and on their noses, they cannot lose heat through sweating like humans. Instead, they pant—the first sign that they need water and shelter from the heat. Remember, if you feel hot and thirsty, most likely your dog does, too. Always provide plenty of fresh drinking water for your dog when spending time outside, and stay inside on especially stifling days.

If you suspect that your Springer is suffering from heatstroke, place the dog in a tub of cool water or gently wrap him in a towel soaked with cold water. Never use ice-cold water. Once your dog's temperature is lowered to 103°F (39°C)—a rectal thermometer can provide you with an accurate reading—seek veterinary care at once.

Encounters with Other Animals and Insects

Bites

Bites from other animals require prompt veterinary attention. Never assume that a neighborhood dog's vaccinations are current. Even if the owner assures you that they are, getting your dog to his vet as quickly as possible will help ensure the best positive outcome.

If a wild animal bites your Springer, your dog must be taken to the vet immediately because of a potentially fatal viral disease called rabies. There is no treatment for rabies, but your

Who to Call

The ASPCA Animal Poison Control Center offers an emergency hotline at 1-888-426-4435. You can call anytime, 24 hours a day, 365 days a year. There is a charge of $50 per case. You will be asked the name and amount of the toxin your dog was exposed to; the length of time that has passed; the breed, age, sex, and weight of your dog; and the symptoms he is displaying. You will also need to provide your name, address, telephone number, and credit card information.

vet may want to give your Springer a rabies booster immediately following a bite by a wild animal. Even if an animal doesn't look rabid, it can still suffer from this deadly disease.

Skunks

If a skunk has merely sprayed your dog, check his eyes. If they are red and watery, your Springer may have been hit directly in the face. Skunk spray will not cause any permanent damage, but it can be very painful and may cause temporary blindness. If your dog has been sprayed in the face, veterinary care should be sought.

Although old-fashioned remedies like bathing your dog in tomato juice or vinegar are still often used to treat skunk odor, they will likely only mask the smell. A better option is bathing your pet in a quart of 3-percent hydrogen peroxide mixed with one-fourth cup of baking soda and a teaspoon of dishwashing liquid. Wet your dog thoroughly before applying the solution, and take care to keep it away from the dog's eyes, nose, and mouth. The mixture will fizz. *This fizz can create pressure and even explode if enclosed in a sealed container, so discard any unused portion of the treatment.*

Stings

Insect stings can be extremely dangerous. Bee and wasp stings in particular can cause very quick and severe reactions, but these effects are even more rapid in small dogs. If your Springer is stung, call your veterinarian at once. Ice can help reduce swelling; a swollen muzzle is often an indication of a bee sting. Keep some children's diphenhydramine (a common antihistamine used to treat allergic reactions) on hand, and ask your vet for the correct dosage for your dog. This medicine could save your dog's life if he experiences a severe reaction to an insect sting.

Eye Injuries

Eye injuries require prompt veterinary care. Abrasions, lacerations, or punctures to the eye will cause your dog to keep the eye tightly closed, so you will unlikely be able to do much to help the dog yourself. If your dog has something stuck in his eye, you may try flushing the area with ocular irrigation fluid or saline solution, but still contact your veterinarian. The vet can tell if the object has caused any scratching of the cornea. If a chemical irritant was involved in the injury, use clean water to flush the eye as much as possible yourself, and bring the dog to your veterinarian as quickly as possible. If both eyes seem to be affected, a chemical irritant is likely the cause of the problem.

Poison

When we think of dangerous canine poisons, a handful of obvious substances stand out among the rest. Chocolate, certain houseplants, and many human medications all certainly top the

You should have the name and number of an emergency animal hospital on file in case something happens to your Springer and he needs immediate medical attention.

list of toxic substances that should never be given to dogs, but we must also remember that poisons don't always have to be swallowed to pose a problem. Toxins can be eaten, inhaled, or absorbed by a dog's skin— sometimes even without an owner's knowledge.

When a previously healthy dog becomes suddenly ill with no apparent explanation, poisoning is frequently suspected. Signs of poisoning may include vomiting, diarrhea, and trembling, but many chemical toxins do not trigger distinctive signs of illness. This makes identification of the toxin nearly impossible in most cases. If you have reason to believe that your dog has been exposed to any kind of poison, seek advice from a qualified professional immediately.

Ipecac syrup can readily induce vomiting, but depending on the type of poisoning, this

Your Springer's First-Aid Kit

The following items should always be kept on hand in the event of a medical emergency:

- antibiotic ointment
- canine first-aid manual
- children's diphenhydramine (antihistamine)
- corn syrup
- cotton swabs
- emergency phone numbers (including poison control, emergency veterinarian, and your dog's regular vet)
- flashlight and batteries
- hydrogen peroxide
- instant ice pack
- ipecac syrup
- liquid bandages
- mineral oil
- nonstick gauze pads, gauze, and tape
- oral syringe or eyedropper
- rectal thermometer
- saline solution
- scissors
- silver nitrate stick
- soap
- styptic powder or pencil
- tweezers
- any other item your veterinarian recommends keeping on hand

You may also want to assemble a portable emergency kit for your dog if you spend a lot of time hiking, camping, or traveling together. With either type of kit, remember to keep an eye on expiration dates and toss any products before they should no longer be used.

might not be prudent. Caustic toxins, such as drain cleaner, can burn the throat a second time when brought back up through the esophagus. If there is any question as to what kind of poison your dog has ingested, wait for instructions from a poison control expert before doing anything.

Trauma

If your dog experiences trauma—a severe injury or shock to the body from a fall or other accident—you must get your dog to a veterinarian as soon as possible. Extreme care must be used when moving an injured animal, so in order to help your dog you must first protect yourself. Injured animals can act aggressively when they are experiencing trauma, and they may not even recognize their beloved owners. You should never get too close to an injured animal's face. Even the friendliest dogs can deliver a serious bite when in pain.

Check for obvious injuries such as bleeding or distorted limbs. If an appendage is bleeding profusely, a rubber band can serve as a makeshift tourniquet in an emergency. If a bone appears to be fractured or broken, use care not to handle it when moving the animal. Very gently move the dog onto a stiff surface, such as a board, if possible. Use this as an impromptu stretcher. A blanket or a coat will suffice if nothing else is available. If you are alone and cannot hold the dog in place, use a belt or rope to secure him for the ride to the veterinary hospital. Use rolled towels or another coat to keep the dog warm and prevent him from moving around. Keep the dog as still as possible.

Hospice Care

Hospice care for human patients has been around for a long time. More recently, though, the veterinary community has begun offering similar services to owners and their terminally ill pets. While many Springer owners opt to euthanize their dogs shortly after an incurable diagnosis is made, other owners prefer letting nature take its course. Also called palliative care, hospice focuses on improving a dog's quality of life through medication, dietary strategies, and human contact. A hospice worker may teach an owner how reduce nausea or improve blood flow and circulation through canine massage. The biggest goal is relaxing pets during their final weeks or days. Even though there is no hope for recovery, hospice provides both dogs and their owners with invaluable time before saying goodbye.

The English Springer Spaniel

ASSOCIATIONS AND ORGANIZATIONS

Registries

American Kennel Club (AKC)
5580 Centerview Drive
Raleigh, NC 27606
Telephone: (919) 233-9767
Fax: (919) 233-3627
E-mail: info@akc.org
www.akc.org

Canadian Kennel Club (CKC)
89 Skyway Avenue, Suite 100
Etobicoke, Ontario M9W 6R4
Telephone: (416) 675-5511
Fax: (416) 675-6506
E-mail: information@ckc.ca
www.ckc.ca

The Kennel Club
1 Clarges Street
London
W1J 8AB
Telephone: 0870 606 6750
Fax: 0207 518 1058
www.the-kennel-club.org.uk

United Kennel Club (UKC)
100 E. Kilgore Road
Kalamazoo, MI 49002-5584
Telephone: (269) 343-9020
Fax: (269) 343-7037
E-mail: pbick-ell@ukcdogs.com
www.ukcdogs.com

RESCUE ORGANIZATIONS AND ANIMAL WELFARE GROUPS

American Humane Association (AHA)
63 Inverness Drive East
Englewood, CO 80112
Telephone: (303) 792-9900
Fax: 792-5333
www.americanhumane.org

American Society for the Prevention of Cruelty to Animals (ASPCA)
424 E. 92nd Street
New York, NY 10128-6804
Telephone: (212) 876-7700
www.aspca.org

Royal Society for the Prevention of Cruelty to Animals (RSPCA)
Telephone: 0870 3335 999
Fax: 0870 7530 284
www.rspca.org.uk

The Humane Society of the United States (HSUS)
2100 L Street, NW
Washington DC 20037
Telephone: (202) 452-1100
www.hsus.org

Sports

American Kennel Club
Agility:
www.akc.org/events/agility/index.cfm

Conformation:
www.akc.org/events/conformation/index.cfm

Obedience:
www.akc.org/events/obedience/index.cfm

Rally:
www.akc.org/events/rally/index.cfm

Tracking:
www.akc.org/events/tracking/index.cfm

American Herding Breeds Association (AHBA)
www.ahba-herding.org

American Mixed Breed Obedience Registry (AMBOR)
www.amborusa.com

Association of Pet Dog Trainers (APDT) Rally
www.apdt.com/po/rally/default.aspx

International Agility Link (IAL)
www.agilityclick.com/~ial

North American Dog Agility Council (NADAC)
www.nadac.com

North American Flyball Association (NAFA)
www.flyball.org

United States Dog Agility Association (USDAA)
www.usdaa.com

Veterinary Resources

Academy of Veterinary Homeopathy (AVH)
P.O. Box 9280
Wilmington, DE 19809
Telephone: (866) 652-1590
Fax: (866) 652-1590
E-mail: office@TheAVH.org
www.theavh.org

American Academy of Veterinary Acupuncture (AAVA)

100 Roscommon Drive, Suite 320
Middletown, CT 06457
Telephone: (860) 635-6300
Fax: (860) 635-6400
E-mail: office@aava.org
www.aava.org

American Animal Hospital Association (AAHA)

P.O. Box 150899
Denver, CO 80215-0899
Telephone: (303) 986-2800
Fax: (303) 986-1700
E-mail: info@aahanet.org
www.aahanet.org/index.cfm

American Holistic Veterinary Medical Association (AHVMA)

2218 Old Emmorton Road
Bel Air, MD 21015
Telephone: (410) 569-0795
Fax: (410) 569-2346
E-mail: office@ahvma.org
www.ahvma.org

American Veterinary Medical Association (AVMA)

1931 North Meacham Road – Suite 100
Schaumburg, IL 60173
Telephone: (847) 925-8070
Fax: (847) 925-1329
E-mail: avmainfo@avma.org
www.avma.org

British Veterinary Association (BVA)

7 Mansfield Street
London
W1G 9NQ
Telephone: 020 7636 6541
Fax: 020 7436 2970
E-mail: bvahq@bva.co.uk
www.bva.co.uk

Training and Behavior Resources

Animal Behavior Society (ABS)

Certified Applied Animal Behaviorist Directory:
www.animalbehavior.org/ABSAppliedBehavior/caab-directory

Association of Pet Dog Trainers (APDT)

150 Executive Center Drive
Box 35
Greenville, SC 29615
Telephone: (800) PET-DOGS
Fax: (864) 331-0767
E-mail: information@apdt.com
www.apdt.com

Certification Council for Professional Dog Trainers (CCPDT)

E-mail: administrator@ccpdt.org
www.ccpdt.org

Animal-Assisted Activities & Therapy Organizations

Delta Society

875 124th Ave NE, Suite 101
Bellevue, WA 98005
Telephone: (425) 226-7357
Fax: (425) 235-1076
E-mail: info@deltasociety.org
www.deltasociety.org

Therapy Dogs, Inc.

P.O. Box 20227
Cheyenne WY 82003
Telephone: 877-843-7364
E-mail: therapy-dogsinc@qwest.net
www.therapydogs.com

Therapy Dogs International, Inc. (TDI)

88 Bartley Road
Flanders, NJ 07836
Telephone: (973) 252-9800
Fax: (973) 252-7171
E-mail: tdi@gti.net
www.tdi-dog.org

PUBLICATIONS

Books

Anderson, Teoti. Terra-Nova *Puppy Care & Training*. Neptune City: T.F.H. Publications, Inc., 2007.

———. *The Super Simple Guide to Housetraining*. Neptune City: T.F.H. Publications, Inc., 2004.

De Vito, Dominique. Animal Planet *Training Your Dog*. Neptune City: T.F.H. Publications, Inc., 2007.

King, Trish. *Parenting Your Dog*. Neptune City: T.F.H. Publications, Inc., 2004.

Yin, Sophia. *How to Behave so Your Dog Behaves*. T.F.H. Publications, Inc., 2004.

Magazines

AKC Family Dog
American Kennel Club
260 Madison Avenue
New York, NY 10016
Telephone: (800) 490-5675
E-mail: familydog@akc.org
www.akc.org/pubs/familydog

AKC Gazette
American Kennel Club
260 Madison Avenue
New York, NY 10016
Telephone: (800) 533-7323
E-mail: gazette@akc.org
www.akc.org/pubs/gazette

Dog Fancy
Subscription Department
P.O. Box 53264
Boulder, CO 80322-3264
Telephone: (800) 365-4421
E-mail: bark-
back@dogfancy.com
www.dogfancy.com

Dogs Monthly
Ascot House
High Street, Ascot,
Berkshire SL5 7JG
United Kingdom
Telephone: 0870 730 8433
Fax: 0870 730 8431
E-mail: admin@rtc-associ-
ates.freeserve.co.uk
www.corsini.co.uk/dogsmont
hly

WEBSITES

www.nylabone.com

www.tfh.com

T

table manners, 75–76
tags, 40
tail, docking of, 13
tattoos as identification mark, 44
temperament and behavior, 14
theobromine, 74–75
Therapy Dogs International (TDI), 149
therapy work, 148–149
thyroid disorders, 170
ticking, on coat, 11
ticks, 181–183
tocopherols as preservatives, 59
toxins, 72, 195–196. *See also* poisoning
   Poison Control Hotline number, 194
   vinyl (PVC) and phthalates as, 42
toys, 40–42, **41**
training, 14, 21, 77, 99–131
   age and, 100
   basic obedience commands in, 112–120
   canine body language, 129
   Canine Good Citizen (CGC) program and, 133–135, 149
   Come command in, 115, **115**
   command words used in, 110
   crates in, 104–108, **105**, **107**
   discipline vs. punishment in, 99
   Down command in, 116–117
   Drop It/Leave It command in, 119–120
   family's role in, 102–104
   field/hunting dogs and, 114
   goals of, 100–101
   Heel command in, 117–119
   housetraining in, 108–111
   importance of, 99–100
   leash in, 111–, 112
   lifetime pursuit of, 130
   off-leash time and, 135
   positive reinforcement in, 101
   problem behaviors and. *See* problem behaviors
   professionals for, 101–102
   puppy kindergarten in, 22
   rewards based, 77
   Sit command in, 116
   socialization in, 26, 103
   Stay command in, 117
   table manners in, 75–76
   treats as rewards in, 77, **115**
tranquilizers, 121
traumatic injuries, 197
traveling with your English Springer Spaniel, 46–47
treats, 74–75
   training using, 77, **115**

U

umbilical hernias, 162

United States and the English Springer Spaniel, 7–8

V

vaccination schedule, 157–159
vegetarian diets, 66
veterinarian selection, 151–155, 199–200
   boarding facilities and, 50
vinyl in dog toys, 42
visiting the breeder, 25
vitamin E, 71
vitamins and minerals, 55, 70–71

W

walking with your English Springer Spaniel, 111–112
   Heel command and, 117–119
Wallace, William, 6
warranties and guarantees, 28
water dishes, 35, **35**
water needs, 56
websites of interest, 15, 201
weight control, 69, 71–75, 176–177
Welsh Springer Spaniel, 6, **7**
Westminster Kennel Club Dog Show, 8, 9
World Canine Freestyle Organization (WCFO), 145
worms and worming, 183–184

DEDICATION
To Molly and Damon

ACKNOWLEDGMENTS

I would like to thank the following breeders for taking the time to speak with me about their experiences with English Springer Spaniels: Susan Campbell, Don & Carol Callahan, Maura Constantine, Lisa Coterillo, Kevin & Barbara Czarzasty, Bobbie Daniel, LeeAnn Gutzwiler, Mark Haglin, Dawn Horock, Dave and Janee' Kemp, Lisa Knight, Judy Manley, Debra Maxwell, Marti Nickoli, Lynda O'Connor, Linda Prouty, Bob Robella, Robert A. Satoloe, Daniel Sena, DDS, Cheryl Sligar, Kathleen Snyder, and Janet Warner.

ABOUT THE AUTHOR

Tammy Gagne is a freelance writer who specializes in the health and behavior of companion animals. In addition to being a regular contributor to several national pet care magazines, she has authored numerous books for both adults and children. She resides in northern New England with her husband, son, dogs, and parrots.

PHOTO CREDITS

Tim Callen (Shutterstock): 75, 142

Denise Campione (Shutterstock): 88

Jeff Dalton (Shutterstock): 5

Trisha Dunn: 4, 12, 16, 20, 22, 26, 32, 35, 37, 41, 43, 45, 63, 84, 90, 98, 100, 106, 107, 111, 132, 136, 158

Isabelle Francais: 7 (left & right), 8 (bottom), 39, 52, 54, 58 (top), 72, 74, 76, 78, 81, 87, 92, 95 (bottom), 96, 102, 104, 115, 116, 124, 130, 147, 165, 171, 179, 188-189, 192, 195, 198, 201

Scot Gagne: 27, 30, 61, 144, 176, 182

Andrew Howard (Shutterstock): 8 (top), 42

HTuller (Shutterstock): 58 (bottom)

Interpet: Front Cover, 10, 15, 18, 23, 48, 49, 55, 56, 65, 67, 70, 73, 83, 109, 113, 118, 120, 122, 126, 128, 134, 148, 150, 152, 155, 164, 168, 172-173, 184, 191

All other photos are courtesy of the TFH Photo Archives

NATURAL with added VITAMINS
Nutri Dent ®MD
Promotes Optimal Dental Health!

Visit
nylabone.com
Join Club NYLA
for coupons &
product
information

360° Design
Cleaning Action!™

Dog's Love 'em!™

AVAILABLE IN MULTIPLE SIZES AND FLAVORS.

Nylabone®

Trusted For Over 40 Years

MADE IN THE USA